Parenting Your Adopted Child

Stephanie E. Siegel, Ph.D.

PARENTING YOUR ADOPTED CHILD

•────────────•

A Complete and Loving Guide

Prentice Hall Press

New York   London   Toronto   Sydney   Tokyo

Prentice Hall Press
Gulf+Western Building
One Gulf+Western Plaza
New York, New York   10023

PRENTICE HALL PRESS and colophon are registered
trademarks of Simon & Schuster, Inc.

Library of Congress Cataloging-in-Publication Data

Siegel, Stephanie E.
  Parenting your adopted child.

  Bibliography: p.
  Includes index.
  1. Adoption—United States.   2. Parenting—
United States.   I. Title.
HV875.55.S57   1989   649'.145   88-19711
ISBN 0-13-815325-6

Designed by Victoria Hartman

Manufactured in the United States of America

10 9 8 7 6 5 4 3 2 1

First Edition

I lovingly dedicate this book to
my husband, Arne, for his encouragement and support;
my children, Carrie, Jonathan, Ethan, and Oren,
for teaching me how to mother;
their biofamilies, for their gift of life;
and adoptive families everywhere.

Acknowledgments

I gratefully acknowledge the following individuals for their contributions to this manuscript: my husband, Arne, for his love, nurturing, and support; my children, Carrie, Jonathan, Ethan, and Oren, for their inspiration from the beginning; the many families who have given me guidance and insight into their lives so that I might help others; Sherry Robb, my literary agent, for her faith in me; PJ Dempsey, my editor at Prentice Hall Press, for her enthusiasm and assistance throughout the project; Maureen Clark, for expert copyediting which maintained the integrity of my book; and Betty Freeman, for her wisdom.

Thank you for making this book possible.

Contents

PART III · DISCOVERING AN IDENTITY

Introduction

I first became interested in the adoption process more than twenty-five years ago. At that time, I had been undergoing the long and painful course of discovering that I was infertile and was looking for alternatives.

When my husband and I married, we assumed that we would have several children. I was teaching and he was completing a master's program, so we decided to wait before starting our family. Two years later, we were ready and confident that our first child would be conceived within a short time.

We were overjoyed at the prospect of becoming parents and, in anticipation of my pregnancy, I began to look for signs that I was actually pregnant. After many months, I called my doctor for an appointment. It was evident that the pregnancy was taking much longer than we had planned. What we did not know then was how much would be involved over the next three years.

Initially, my husband and I were both examined, but it was soon very clear that I was the one with the problem. I was still hopeful and felt encouraged, with each medical procedure, that I would soon be pregnant. Of course, it would happen. Look at all of the expectant couples among our friends, neighbors, and family. The whole world was pregnant, or so it seemed to me.

At family gatherings, people would ask, "And when will a little one be coming along?" Our parents would say, "We can't wait to be grandparents." These questions and statements were reminders of our inability to make it happen. I resented their comments and felt intruded upon, though their expectations were certainly normal and mirrored our own.

It was then that I decided to tell the truth about my infertility. As I began talking about it, I realized how much pain I had been carrying within me. Along with the hurt were tears of mourning for the child I might never have. I felt guilty that I was the "problem." Even though my husband was very supportive, I believed that I carried the burden of our infertility. I should have been able to make it happen.

During the mourning period, I continued the medical treatment. Initial hope had turned first to discouragement and then to a useless routine. I went through the motions of treatment, but my heart was no longer in it. I was depressed and felt useless.

Sometime during my third year of treatment, my doctor suggested that my husband and I consider adopting a child. There was still no conclusive evidence that I was infertile, but I certainly was not pregnant. My husband had talked about adoption several years earlier, but I had never considered it seriously. Determined to conceive, I was not ready to give up. Even though I spoke freely about my infertility, I had not worked it through sufficiently to accept adoption.

Shortly thereafter, I received a phone call from my doctor: He knew of a baby who would be placed for adoption at birth. My husband was eager to take the child, but I could not commit myself. I was still in conflict over wanting to give birth to my own child. Another couple adopted that baby.

Although I'm not exactly sure when it happened, one day I knew I was ready. My anger, tears, and depression had passed, and I was certain I wanted to adopt a child. My desire to become a mother was greater than my need to bear a child. I left my sorrow behind. The second part of the adoption process could now begin.

We contacted the local county agency and were invited to an orientation for prospective adopting couples. As the process continued, we discovered the meaning of adoption. At each meeting with our adoption worker, we learned more about adoption and more about ourselves. We knew that we were being not only evaluated as potential parents but also prepared emotionally for parenthood. (Fertile couples prepare for their role as parents during the nine months of pregnancy.)

About a year after the initial orientation, we received a call from our adoption worker: Our daughter had arrived and we could bring her home the next day. In a flurry of excitement, we made the final preparations for her welcome. It was as if she had always been waiting there just for us.

We adopted our second child, a son, sixteen months later, and another son two years after that. A third son was born to us a couple of years later. Although our biological child was a surprise, he readily became a part of our family, joining his brothers and sister. Family ties—adopted or biological—are powerful.

As my family grew, I became aware of the special needs of the adoptive family. I could see that we were unique as a family and as individuals. Each of my children had brought to our family his or her own style of relating to the world. My husband and I had questions about the heritage and background of our children, but there were few clues to help us. I longed for guidance, for some assistance along the way. We dearly loved our children but knew so little about them.

As I experienced the day-by-day demands of being an adoptive mother, I came to realize that the ways I found to deal with our practical problems could help others. When my youngest son started school, I began my graduate studies to become a family therapist—an infertility and adoption specialist. During those years, I continued to learn from my children; by the time I completed my doctoral dissertation and clinical internship, I was confident that I could help adoptive families.

Since then, I have counseled hundreds of individuals, families, and groups—infertile couples, adopting couples, adoptive families, adoptees young and old, bioparents—both in my private practice and in the community. I have often been consulted about search and reunion issues.

Although many infertile couples create a family through adoption, other couples choose to adopt a child even though they are fertile. Infertile couples with adopted children face the same issues that all adoptive parents must confront, and they must also cope with the inability to conceive. This book deals with relevant issues specific to infertile couples. It is important to remember that adoption itself is always a major theme for adoptive families, no matter what is the initial motivation to adopt. This book is for *all* adoptive families. I will share with you my personal and clinical experiences and offer guidance, comfort, and practical solutions for families just like mine.

The material for this book comes from my work with adoptive families: Whenever particular situations are described, the names and events have been changed to protect the privacy of those families. Incidents you read about in these pages may be very much like your own experiences, however, because all adoptive families have a great deal in common.

I use the words *bioparents, biomother,* and *biofather* to identify the biological families of adopted children. These terms and others are defined more fully in appendix A.

I

Having a Child to Love

1

Life's Inalienable Right

"When I grow up, I'm going to get married and have babies, just like Mommy and Daddy."

Do you remember saying that when you were a child? Perhaps you "played house" with a friend. One of you would be Daddy and the other, Mommy. More than likely, Mommy would be pregnant. She might even put a pillow under her dress to be as authentic as possible and capture the full effect of the fantasy. Miraculously, the baby would be born, and you would spend hours caring for your baby doll.

For most children the reality of birth is very much like the fantasy. When Mommy or a relative is pregnant, children will watch in awe as tummies enlarge to accommodate the growing baby. To feel a brother kicking or hear a sister's heartbeat is an amazing phenomenon for the young child. In your own childhood, you may have been delighted at the arrival of a new baby so that you could have a real baby doll to care for.

The wonder of birth engrosses all of us.

Society's Claim on Fertility

Most people take fertility for granted. They expect to conceive and bear children as their parents, family, and friends did. When a couple marries, it is assumed that they will someday

3

have a family. Child-bearing and child-rearing are tasks they eagerly expect to accomplish. Their childhood hopes and dreams now can be realized.

Married couples are entrusted with hope and promise through their offspring. By bearing children, they pass on the family legacy to future generations. When couples consciously decide to start a family, they unconsciously bring to that plan all of their own expectations, as well as those of their family and society. The unborn child is endowed with traits to endure all obstacles and to accomplish all incomplete dreams.

It's no small task.

In many instances, the married couple is *expected* to create the ideal child. For some families, it is considered the duty of the son to produce a male heir who will carry on the family name. We all know a John Jr. or a Thomas II or a Matthew III, for example. These children not only assume the family name but also, in some cases, become their parents' and grandparents' second chance. They are either supposed to compensate for what is lacking in their forefathers or to grow up and be just like them. The shoes of their grandfathers and fathers are ready to be worn, even if they don't fit.

All Grown Up

Fertility is usually the indication that adulthood has arrived—the official sign of having grown up. When a woman becomes pregnant, she is able to reinforce her self-image as a female. Many women feel fulfilled and complete when they are expecting a child. They believe that they have something in common with other women, particularly their own mothers. In a sense, childbirth becomes the culmination of a woman's childhood.

The expectant father has confirmed his self-image of "being a man." His status as an adult male is firmly established now that he has something in common with all men, particularly his own father. He believes that he has unqualified proof of his virility and manliness. When he hands out cigars at the time of his baby's birth, he further cements the bond of fatherhood.

Basic Biology

Along with growing up comes that basic biological motivation to reproduce offspring. An internal instinctual energy drives us to parenting. We are not only impelled to survive but also moved to nurture. Our desire to shelter and care for our young appears to be more than society's example. We welcome our role as protector and guardian and never consider that anything could interfere with conceiving and bearing a child.

Then we discover that we are infertile.

The Infertile Couple

If you are infertile, you face one of life's most painful circumstances. You experience overwhelming feelings that are difficult to endure. Other people will not be able to relate to your problem. You, too, will not fully understand what is taking place. With each piece of confirming evidence, you will want to deny the reality and make it go away. How could that be happening to you?

Instead of looking forward to the exciting prospect of bearing a child, you now carry a burden that your family and friends cannot understand. Your infertility has become a betrayal of your family's wishes. Intense feelings of shame and guilt may consume you, and it will be difficult to talk to anyone about your predicament. I remember how those emotions depleted my energy as I tried to hide from the truth. Then I realized that if I did not attempt to talk about my misfortune, no one would really understand, and I would not get the support and empathy I so desperately needed.

Under these enormous pressures, you may at first rationalize that you are not ready to have a family. This works for a while.

During the course of your medical treatment, some of you may be able to conceive a child, only to miscarry during the pregnancy. Repeated miscarriages are the most difficult form of infertility to explain and to deal with. Every conception generates new hope, which is then destroyed within a few months.

After your first miscarriage, you become wary and reserve your enthusiasm. Each hopeful pregnancy and subsequent miscarriage serve to reinforce feelings of hopelessness. At times, you probably want to scream in outrage.

Burdens on the Marriage

Infertility knows no gender. Both men and women can be infertile and may feel singled out and alone, not only among family and friends but also within the marriage. After all, no couple wants to be told that they can't produce a child and neither partner wants to be the one responsible. It is difficult to accept that fact.

Your feelings as a couple are so important. As you try to cope with infertility, tensions can mount in your marriage; communication can be blocked. It's hard to talk when the cloud of infertility is hanging over you. Exaggerated feelings of inadequacy will often accompany the problem, interfering with and inhibiting your sexual relationship. Once warm and loving feelings become strained and lifeless and lack spontaneity.

Then you find a solution.

Letting Go of the Dream

All of us who want a child and have been diagnosed as infertile reach a point when we have had enough. We realize that family and friends care about us but are not able to help. We have to deal with our own feelings.

Sure, there are times when we receive a baby announcement, send a baby gift, or visit a new baby and are reminded of our infertility. Each incident is chalked up as either a major blow or a minor twinge, depending on how well we are coping that day. It seems babies are everywhere: gurgling in carriages being pushed by their mothers, crying in supermarket shopping carts. Our friends may be expecting a baby, and we feel either envious or resentful. We see pregnant women beaming with pride.

Then, one day, we all begin to let go.

One morning, I awoke and became aware of the fact that it had been some time since I had cried or been outraged about my infertility. I discovered that I could move beyond my infertility and still have my family.

2

Adoption: Your Choice

Your decision to adopt a child was made after a long and emotional period. Some of you may have chosen to adopt even though you are fertile, but most of you had to overcome and work through powerful feelings about your infertility with little support. Family and friends may have wanted to empathize with you but lacked the experience and understanding to do so.

The Decision to Adopt

Most people are not able to identify with the decision to adopt. The preparation for biological parenting is usually done with ease and familiarity. Family and friends rejoice and look forward with enthusiasm to the potential offspring.

This is not the experience of most adopting couples.

Congratulations and compliments are not always in the offing. Instead, you may receive pity and consolation when you announce your plans. The negative comments and attitudes remind you that you are different from other couples:

"Oh, you're so lucky. You won't have to go through painful labor."

"As soon as you adopt, you'll get pregnant."

"Are you really sure you can't have a child of your own?"

"Why did you decide to do this?"

With each remark, you are confronted with your dissimilarity. As adoptive parents, you will probably continue to hear similar comments from people who are unable to relate to adoption. In time, however, you will be better able to deal with the remarks.

Society's Attitudes

A great deal of discrimination and prejudice surrounds the child who has been relinquished for adoption and the bioparents of that child. A few married couples will give up a child for adoption, but the majority of relinquishments are the result of a relationship "out of wedlock." In either case, society does not generally support these decisions.

Even though sexual attitudes have changed in recent years, most people are unable to accept the primary source of adopted children. Community viewpoints stress the risks involved in adoption and the great social responsibility of the adoptive parents. Society focuses on adoption as a way to save a poor child from a bleak fate rather than as a way to save an infertile couple from childlessness.

Adoption is looked upon as a "good deed," and it seems as if that is the only way it can be understood and rationalized by others.

If a child is placed for adoption by a married couple, their motivation will be questioned:

"How can they give up their baby?"
"Why is this child unwanted?"
"What's wrong with the child or parents?"
"Are you sure you want to adopt *this* child?"

With each question, you feel a need to justify your intention. You may become defensive because these questions probably reflect your own doubts and fears. Your biological child would have been accepted by family and friends without question, but for many of you, your decision to adopt may be tolerated only with reservation. It's as if you have to prove yourself and your resolve.

Yet, despite the long process of mourning your infertility and the adversity, you still choose to adopt a child. Your desire to become parents has been so great that you are able to withstand the questioning and concern of others, as well as your own anxieties.

No doubt, you can still remember what it was like during the painful times and how you overcame your doubts and fears to become the parents you deserve to be. You know how thrilling that first glance at *your child* can be.

The Arrival

I can recall the time when my husband and I adopted our first child. About a year after our initial orientation for adopting couples, we received a call from our adoption worker: Our daughter had arrived and we could bring her home the next day. In a flurry of excitement, we made the final preparations for her welcome.

And then the time came. . . . The two of us sat waiting for our first child. The door opened. Someone brought a pink bundle over to me and placed it in my arms.

I could feel the warmth of the tiny body. I touched the small fist and watched as the baby's hand curled around my finger. Dark lashes touched pink cheeks; silky black hair softened the baby's head. Her eyes opened and met my eyes, and then the eyes of her father. In that moment she was our child.

Had she always been waiting there just for us?

She was ours. There was no doubt about it. How beautiful she was. We left for home that day with information about her feeding schedule and formula and a few facts about her history. Now we were a family.

We began the care of our daughter with an enormous energy and enthusiasm. We called our family and close friends, mailed announcements, and looked forward to opportunities to show her off. Wasn't she wonderful, beautiful, special? Our pleasure was contagious and soon everyone was rejoicing.

As our family and friends met our daughter, they admired her beauty, alertness, and disposition. Of course, we would be marvelous parents, and she would fulfill all of their expectations and ours. We were determined not to repeat the mistakes of our parents and grandparents. We would be model parents to our model child.

Our daughter was our vision of hope.

II

The Growing Child

3

And Baby Makes Three

All couples experience a rebalancing of their lives when a baby arrives. For adoptive parents, however, the infant has an even greater impact.

> The stroller entered my office first, almost propelled by its own power. Lois followed, her hands gripping the handle. She appeared weary. Bob was the last to enter, barely able to get through the door with a diaper bag on one arm, a pink-and-blue blanket on the other, and a half-full baby bottle held somewhere in between. His gray suit looked out of place in the procession.
>
> I smiled at Eric, who was asleep in the stroller, a peaceful look of contentment on his round face. Then I observed his parents: Lois's brown eyes were tired; they lacked the brightness I remembered. I noticed that Bob glanced around my office, shifting in his chair before he spoke.
>
> "Having a baby is not what we thought it would be. Lois is exhausted. There seems to be no relief. We have no time for each other. It's as if an intruder has come into our lives. How do other parents do it?"

As I listened to them, I watched Lois's tense, always-on-the-alert glances at the baby, and I sensed that she was probably undergoing a change that many adoptive parents experience.

Lois and Bob had waited for years to become a family. Now that it had finally happened, they wanted to be sure that nothing would change. Their baby was like a precious prize they had won after a long ride on an obstacle course.

You, too, must know how the prolonged treatment for your infertility delayed your decision to adopt and the many years it took before your child finally arrived in your home. You and your spouse had those years to adjust and accommodate each other's needs, establishing a comfortable relationship. Over a period of time, a sense of stability evolved around you both as a couple. Each partner learned about the other, and understanding and mutual respect developed.

This new addition simply upsets the balance.

Rebalancing Your Lives

A baby brings a new dimension to your functioning as a couple. A tiny third party is suddenly tugging and pulling at you, taking time and energy, driving a wedge between you. Under these circumstances, it is not uncommon to feel overwhelmed by the demands of a new baby.

In reality, this baby is invading an established relationship.

Other reasons contribute to the difficulty of adjusting to this new family setup.

Uncertainties and anxieties are part of the parenting process for *all* new parents. Even though most first-time parents are determined to do a good job, their intensity may get in the way and make the task more difficult.

The first child in families usually carries most of the burden of the parents' expectations about child-rearing. New parents are usually overly conscientious and intense about raising their first child. Through inexperience and feelings left over from childhood, they may develop rigid standards for themselves. They are well aware of the mistakes of their parents and have no desire to repeat them.

Trial and error is part of *all* parenting experiences. Parents are poorly informed to begin the major responsibility of raising a child.

How to Restore Balance

Always keep the following in mind:

- You as a couple are the foundation of your family.
- Time for you is essential.
- The needs of your baby are important, but you have needs, too.
- Self-sacrifice does not make for good parenting.
- The notion of being a perfect parent is only a fantasy.

When you as an adoptive couple begin your roles as parents, you, too, are confronted with fears and uncertainties. You are eager to be the very best parents, to raise the best children possible, and you are as ill-equipped as any other first-time parents for the task ahead. Your delight at the prospect of parenting and nurturing will be your initial inspiration, but it is not enough.

Adoptive parents, unlike biological parents, deal with far more complex issues.

Infertility Revisited

Although some of you have chosen adoption even though you are able to bear children, most of you adopted a child because you are infertile. It is sometimes difficult to accept the fact that you could have been childless if it were not for adoption. You may love your baby but still have trouble coming to terms with your infertility. Until you are able to resolve those nagging feelings, your relationship with your spouse and your child will suffer.

To determine where you are in your acceptance of your infertility, fill out the following Infertility Checklist.

Infertility Checklist

	Yes	No
Do you find yourself wondering if the bio-mother could do it better?	_____	_____

Do you believe that you were not meant to be a parent because of your infertility? _____ _____

Do you always compare yourself to parents of biological children? _____ _____

When your child cries and you are not able to be comforting, do you question your right to be a parent? _____ _____

Do you deny your feelings of frustration and fatigue at the end of the day, seeing them as signs that you should not have been a parent? _____ _____

When family or friends question your parenting style, do your own doubts consume you? _____ _____

Do you often fantasize about a biological child? _____ _____

Do you become defensive when you are asked if you are breast-feeding your baby? _____ _____

When you think about being infertile, do you feel defective? _____ _____

Has your infertility become a gnawing issue in your daily life? _____ _____

Do you often try to prove that you are a perfect parent with a perfect baby? _____ _____

Do you feel ashamed of being infertile? _____ _____

Do you become angry or sad when you see a pregnant woman? _____ _____

Does your infertility get in your way of being a potentially effective parent?

Answering "yes" to any of the checklist questions indicates that you have not completely accepted your infertility. If the answers to several or all of the questions were "yes," you are setting yourself up for failure and burn-out as a parent.

How to Break Through the Infertility Trap

- Verbalize your feelings about your infertility so that you may begin to deal with them.
- Expect to be ill at ease as a new parent.
- Accept the fact that you will not know all there is to know about infants and their care.
- Believe in yourself.
- Trust your instincts, your intuition about your child.
- Don't allow the opinions of others to be more important than your own.
- Don't let the questions of family and friends interfere with your parenting decisions.
- Accept the fact that you will make mistakes as a parent.
- Know that you are *real* parents with a *real* child.
- Trust in your capacity to be a good parent even though you are infertile.

Now read the Infertility Checklist again.

Were your answers somewhat different the second time? Did you feel differently about infertility? Wait six months and go over the list again. You will probably be surprised to see more "no" answers.

As you begin to believe in yourself and develop more assurance as a parent, your feelings about infertility should change. If infertility still haunts you after six months or a year, however, you may want to consider some sessions with a therapist or counselor. There may be underlying issues motivating you that will require a more in-depth appraisal.

Once you are free of your infertility hang-up, you will be open to a more intense bonding with your child. Unfortunately, infertility is not the only factor that interferes with parent-child bonding in adoptive families.

Waiting for the Adoption to Be Final

When your child is placed in your home, you know that it will be some time before the legal adoption takes place. This is yet another waiting period in the long chain of delays. Even though it is more likely than not that the adoption will be finalized, you will not experience a sense of security until your child is legally yours.

I can vividly recall that block of time after our daughter was placed with us. She was five weeks old when she became a part of our family. It was difficult to believe that we would have to wait for a court date to make her legally ours. She was already our child. How could some legal document have so much control over our lives?

My husband and I experienced increased joy daily as we got to know our daughter. Those first few months were sheer delight, and we never considered that anything could possibly change that.

Then our adoption worker made a home visit. I had believed that this would be a perfunctory call to complete the case and file the necessary papers with the court. Yet, why was I so anxious? I puffed up the cushions and checked for dust at least a dozen times. The house was spotless.

As soon as the doorbell rang, my daughter began to cry and continued to do so until the adoption worker left. Nothing I could do comforted her. She did not respond to any of my usual hugging, patting, rocking, or loving. The adoption worker continued to chat with me, seemingly oblivious to my daughter's cries. I was devastated and half-expected her to take my daughter from me right then. When she finally left, I breathed a sigh of relief, although I wondered when she would return to whisk my baby away. As soon as the door closed, my daughter uttered a few whimpers and then smiled at me. I'm now convinced that my anxiety contributed to her discomfort.

We managed to get past that event and, to my relief, I soon

found out that the petition had been filed with the court and a date was pending. The adoption was finalized two months later. I felt more secure, however, when the amended birth certificate arrived six weeks later.

It is not very easy to develop a strong bond with your child before the legal adoption has taken place. You may attempt to deny your feelings and anxieties, hoping they will go away; you may develop a bravado to disguise your uncertainty; or try to disclaim your fears even though you may be feeling a sense of impermanence with each day that passes until the adoption is final. Many of you will want to avoid all reminders of the incomplete adoption so that your anxieties will not be aroused.

How can you go about protecting yourself from the anguish of uncertainty?

•ACCEPT YOUR FEELINGS.
They won't go away.
•CONSIDER THIS WAITING PERIOD AS DIFFERENT FROM THE PRE-ADOPTION PERIOD.
You already have your child. This wait primarily involves paperwork and legal procedures.
•KNOW THAT YOU ARE DOING EVERYTHING YOU CAN TO SPEED THINGS ALONG.
Develop a checklist of items that need to be completed. Be sure to telephone your attorney and adoption worker from time to time to determine what has been done and what is unfinished.

Although you may not be able to avoid your feelings of irresolution until your baby becomes yours legally, you can still emotionally accept your child as your very own. The bond that is forming between you will grow and will be greatly enriched each day you are together.

There are times, however, when no matter what you do the bioparent may have a change of heart before the adoption is finalized.

If the Bioparent Wants Your Child Returned

When children are placed by an agency, the screening is usually done prior to placement, and it is a *rare* event when a child is taken back. The risk may be greater with an independent adoption; occasionally, a biomother does change her mind, usually within the first few weeks after placement. Less frequently, the claim is made after many months.

The return of a child is a traumatic event for the adoptive parents. Most people are unable to relate to this situation as a real loss. The responses are usually shallow and lack understanding.

> Samantha was with Joan and Bill for several weeks when they were faced with the possibility of her biomother wanting her back. They anguished over the chance of losing their child. Family and friends offered little consolation to them: "It's for the best. Don't fight it." No one could really relate to what they were experiencing. Even Joan's mother said, "Of course she wants her back. After all, it is *her* child."
>
> Joan and Bill felt alone and isolated. No one could empathize with them.
>
> If a young infant were to develop a life-threatening illness and the chance for recovery was slim, most persons would understand. Joan and Bill were facing the imminent loss of their child, Samantha. They were dealing with a life-and-death issue.
>
> Fortunately, after several days of agonizing, the biomother decided not to go ahead with her intention and Samantha "survived."

What are your options when the bioparent wants your child back?

•YOU MAY HIRE AN ATTORNEY.
Set a court date and allow a judge to determine whether you will retain custody of your child.

If the bioparent is unable to afford an attorney, the court will appoint one to represent him or her. (Biofathers may also want their children returned.)

Usually the court appoints an attorney for your child as well.

Although there have been some landmark cases, most decisions are in favor of the bioparent. Most often these cases drag through the courts for many years with enormous emotional and financial cost.

The adoption is not final until a court decision has been made. These cases only determine custody. In the few cases where the adoptive couple is awarded custody, a petition is then filed with the court for the legal adoption.

•YOU MAY RETURN THE CHILD TO THE BIOPARENT.

Be prepared for a period of grieving following the separation from and loss of your child. If you exercise this option, the sooner you do this, the better it will be for you and the child.

You will probably receive little empathy from family and friends because they cannot relate to your situation. They will tell you, "It's probably for the best" or "Don't worry, you'll get another child."

Neither of these choices seems viable but they are the only ones available to you. Carefully consider the ramifications of each before making a decision.

It is important to remember that in the majority of cases, your child's bioparent will not change her mind and you will not be forced to make a choice.

Once your child is yours legally, you may want to deny all of the difficulties of the past and pretend that you are not adoptive parents. For many of you it's like a fairy tale.

The Honeymoon Phase

During the honeymoon period of adoptive parenting, you will not want to consider the problems you may face in the future. You may believe that you will never have issues to deal with and, even if you do, you do not want to face that eventuality while you are in a state of such bliss. Ecstatic, you will probably trust that your love for your child will be great enough to thwart all obstacles to your goal of being a capable parent.

The earlier you can take your head out of the clouds, however, the sooner you will be able to deal with problems as they arise. Those of you who are able to look objectively at your position as adoptive parents will usually begin the job of parenting with more realistic goals for yourself and your child.

Carrying Out Your Parenting Goals

1. ACCEPT THE FACT THAT YOUR ADOPTIVE FAMILY IS DIFFERENT FROM OTHER FAMILIES.

Then you will be able to set realistic goals for yourself as a parent and for your child as an individual. In your desire to be like everyone else, you may close yourself to listening to your child's needs and uniqueness. By trying to be like other families, you will be interfering most with what you want—to be an effective parent.

Once you have taken the first step, the remaining five will be that much easier to accomplish.

2. BE OPEN TO LEARNING ABOUT WHO YOUR CHILD IS.

Your child is a unique individual. If you are open to listening when your baby speaks to you, you will have a great deal of information to help you set realistic goals as a parent.

3. FULLY ACCEPT YOUR BABY.

As you listen and learn, you will be getting acquainted with a very special human being.

4. ABANDON UNREALISTIC EXPECTATIONS.

As you get to know your child, you will realize what will not work.

5. SET REALISTIC GOALS.

This will become easier over time as you follow steps one through four.

6. ALLOW THE BONDS OF ATTACHMENT BETWEEN YOU AND YOUR BABY TO GROW AND DEVELOP.

Fully live and love each day.

As adoptive parents, you will be dealing with your different-ness in many ways. Your baby has come to you with a whole set of unknowns. Your child's temperament, personality, and heredity will often be strikingly different from your own. Your baby's genetic heritage and developmental timetable is unique. Your parenting and the environment can only modify what your child is already predisposed to be.

The journey to identity starts in infancy. You are beginning the process of discovery with your child. As you receive and decode the messages your baby sends you, you will be better able to understand and accept his or her uniqueness. Even though you and your baby are not alike genetically, the emotional bond between you can be very intense. You will get to know and love a very special person.

Talking About Adoption

While you and your baby get acquainted, you will encounter further reminders of how different you are from other families. During this time, you will probably wonder about how to tell your child about adoption so that you can eventually foster an open and honest dialogue.

The Telling

When your children are infants:

PRACTICE USING THE WORD *ADOPTION.*

This will give you an opportunity to get used to saying the word without awkwardness or discomfort. You can say "We're so happy we adopted you" while you are hugging and holding your baby. "We're so lucky to have adopted you into our family" is an alternative.

USE THE WORD AT A TIME WHEN YOU FEEL CLOSE TO YOUR CHILD.

Holding, diapering, bathing are all possible situations.

USE THE WORD *ADOPTION* SPONTANEOUSLY.

Don't preplan. Don't schedule regular intervals of time. Don't focus on the word. Say it infrequently when it seems natural to do so.

Infancy sets the stage for open communication about adoption. Be honest with yourself so that you can be honest with your children. You are an *adoptive* family and you can't change that fact. Your children have a right to know as much as possible concerning their backgrounds and adoption. If you attempt to hide the facts from them, they will feel deceived and betrayed by you when they ultimately find out (and they will).

It is also very difficult to hide from your family and friends the fact that you have adopted a child. They will want to know about the adoption and will have many questions.

As questions are asked about your child, consider these three factors:

1. It is up to you to decide what information you want to share or are obligated to share. New adoptive parents tend to give out a great deal of information initially.

2. Before you share any information, determine whether it is in the best interests of you or your child and what benefit it will serve. Your family and friends may be curious about your child. They may mean well, but *you* must decide who knows about the adoption and what they know. It may not be in your child's best interests for everyone to be told. Of course, family and close friends will know, but is it necessary to share that information with anyone else?

3. Take into account who is asking the question or needs to know. It is certainly important to let your child's physician know about prenatal care, delivery, and all background health information that you have about your child's biological family. Either the agency or the bioparents should provide you with this information during the preadoption interview process. You have a right to know as much as possible.

When you first adopt, you may want to tell everyone everything about your child to show that you have made a great choice. You may believe that you need to justify the adoption by making your child the proof of your good judgment.

The real issue, however, is how the "telling" will affect your children. View your babies within the concept of a life cycle. As your children grow older, they will talk about adoption. If they learn about it from you, and you are comfortable with it, they will talk about it themselves. They will do the "telling" when they believe it's appropriate.

Guidelines for Talking About Adoption

- Respect your child's and your own rights to privacy.
- Decide *who* needs to know *what.*
- Acknowledge the natural curiosity of others.
- Accept the fact that others will question you.
- Expect everyone to be uninformed and ignorant about adoption.
- Educate others about adoption in general, *not* about your child in particular.

You do not have to justify anything about your family to anyone.

Here is one mother's story:

> Pam was a new adoptive mother of a baby girl. She was in the supermarket one day when a checker looked at her infant and asked, "Where did she get those beautiful long lashes?" Pam was taken aback by the question, and for a moment considered telling the checker that her daughter was adopted and that the long lashes were inherited from her biomother. She finally said, however, "They are beautiful, aren't they?" Then she walked out of the store with her groceries and her infant with the beautiful eyelashes.

Pam decided rightly that she was not obligated to share private family matters with a stranger.

Let's see how Jeff, an adoptive father of two sons, handled some probing queries.

> When Jeff took his two boys to the park, another parent asked, "Are they brothers? They certainly don't look

it. Who do they resemble?'' Jeff answered, ''Yes, they are special individuals, and I enjoy them both.''

Jeff did not believe that he had to justify his children's appearance to anyone.

Here are some of the most commonly asked questions and suggested answers:

Q. What do you know about her real mother?
A. We are her real parents, *or*
If you mean her biomother, that's private information for our daughter only.
Q. Where did he get that blond hair?
A. He was born that way, *or*
We think that he's so handsome with that hair color.
Q. Where did she get those beautiful eyes and long lashes?
A. They are beautiful, aren't they?
Q. I can't believe how much he resembles you. Don't you agree?
A. That's what everyone says.
Q. Who does she look like?
A. She looks like herself.

You may also beam with pride as an answer to any of the above questions.

You will also want to protect your child from the intrusiveness of others; however, you probably will not be successful. Adoption is an important part of your life and the life of your child, and questions from others are part of the package. As you become more comfortable as an adoptive parent, you will be more at ease. Your child and others will pick up the cues from you.

The Inevitable Separation from Your Baby

In your attempt to shield your children, you may be overprotective to the point of not allowing anyone else to care for them.

Many adoptive parents try to hang on to their children for fear of losing them. You may also be anxious about someone whisking your baby away from you if you are not there. Waiting so long for a child can create profound worries about any separation. Yet, being apart is inevitable and from time to time it will be necessary to be away from your child. To plan for a successful separation:

• Believe that you need time alone and with your spouse. (Remember the *balance* we talked about earlier.)
• Understand your own feelings about separation.
• Know that your baby will be *safe and secure with a competent baby-sitter.* Set up short times away at first. Contact other families, local schools, churches, temples, and community centers for recommendations, and ask for references. Gradually build up a list of reliable baby-sitters. Of course, ask grandparents when they are available.
• Consider that when you leave your children, they learn how to cope and deal with the world even though you are not there.

Now let's look at separation from a different vantage point.

When the Older Infant Is Adopted

If you have adopted an "older infant" (ages six months to two years) it is important to consider four factors:

1. THIS CHILD WILL HAVE MEMORY TRACES OF PAST CARETAKERS.

Because your child is preverbal, these memories will be at a feeling level. He will be afraid of you at first. Expect wariness. Handle him gently, with sure hands and steady movements. Use a calm, soft voice when talking to him.

2. THIS CHILD WILL GO THROUGH A MOURNING PHASE AFTER BEING PLACED WITH YOU.

The extent of and time for the grieving will depend on her age at placement. Be prepared for fussiness, crying, wakefulness during the night, and poor appetite at times.

Hold, cuddle, and nurture your baby through this period. You are creating a comfortable and safe place for her.

3. A READJUSTMENT PHASE WILL FOLLOW IN WHICH THIS CHILD WILL BEGIN TO TEST HIS NEW SURROUNDINGS.

He may test his limits with extensive crying periods, or he may aggressively explore his new environment. You must let him know his boundaries, and, with a gentle consistency, discipline him whenever necessary. This will allay his anxiety and your own and it will also help him create appropriate behavior and boundaries.

During this time, you will be learning about him, his needs, and who he is, and he will learn more about you; it's a getting-acquainted period.

4. A NATURAL EMOTIONAL BONDING WILL TAKE PLACE.

These four factors also apply to infants as young as a few days old. The younger the infant is when placed with you, the shorter and easier the transition will be. Of course, the very young infant will not be crawling and walking about, and you will not be setting limits as you would for an older child.

As you move along on your journey as adoptive parents, trust in your own judgment. Be honest with yourself. You are and will always be an adoptive family, but you are also the true parents of your adopted child.

4

The Terrific and Terrible Toddler

The preschool "toddler" years are difficult ones for all parents. In a very short time, your children will change from helpless infants into active youngsters ready to explore, challenge, and test the world. Each day will become an exciting adventure for them. As they discover their environment, they will also learn more about themselves.

As parents, you will become observing participants in this process. As you get to know more about your youngsters and how to best meet their needs you will teach them how to set controls and limits for themselves. Your adoptive family will have special needs at this time.

The experiments and explorations of your toddlers will serve as ways to give them more information about their surroundings. Inquisitiveness will take form through both action and language. In an effort to make sense of happenings and events, toddlers will physically explore and verbally question the "why" and "how" of things.

Your Children's Very Own Adoption Story

This is the period in your children's development when you can begin a true dialogue about adoption. You have already prepared for this moment by using the word *adoption* and telling them how delighted you were in having adopted them.

Now you can develop the story further and give them more details about the occasion. Each adoptive family has a unique adoption story; however, you should include the following important elements:

• Be sure that your children know that they were *born* first and then you adopted them. Many adopted youngsters believe that other children are born and that they were not born, only adopted. Your boys and girls must understand that everyone is born.

• Describe what they looked like when you first saw them. Focus on outstanding features, what they were wearing, how they smiled at you.

• Tell them how you felt when you first saw them.

• Describe what it was like when you finally held them in your arms.

• Fill them in on all of the details about their trip home with you. Describe their room, their bed, their very own things.

• Point out how exceptional their arrival was and who came to the house to meet them. ,

• Show them snapshots and photos of your family on that extraordinary day. You may also want to include photos of grandparents and close friends of the family.

• Remember that adoption is a memorable occasion and should be treated as such. A *birthday,* however, is the *day* to be celebrated each year. Do not confuse your children by celebrating their adoption day as well.

All children want to hear this special story over and over again. You will be close to one another during these times, and they will set the foundation for future communication and dialogue about all significant events. You will be indicating to this small person that he or she is free to talk to you, and you will listen.

With each "telling" of this adoption story, children frequently ask you to repeat some parts and want to know more details about others. You may have more information than they are able to handle now, and you will have to decide at what later age to discuss these facts.

Your child's very own adoption story is meant to act as a way of bringing you closer together, and it will reinforce how much he or she was wanted and accepted by you. It should give both of you a strong sense of security, safety, and warmth and deepen the understanding of how much you belong to each other.

There may be times when it is difficult to consider that your child is adopted. As you grow closer together and the emotional and psychological bonds are strengthened, you may wonder if there was ever a time when you were not together. It will seem as if your child were always your child. There will be few memories of those years when you were childless, waiting for this moment of actually having a child to love.

You may want to forget about adoption and pretend that this is your biological child. It would certainly be easier not to have to deal with the "telling" or answering questions. You might even be able to convince yourself that you could get away with it, keep the secret.

Unfortunately, the secret would be kept only from your children. Other people already know about the adoption, and a high price is paid for attempting to conceal knowledge of such significance. When your children do find out, and they will, the feelings of rage and betrayal will be so profound that they will severely wound, interfere with, and perhaps sever any relationship you ever had with them. They have a right to know. Who is better able to share that information with them than you, the parents who raise them, love them, and care the most about them?

So it is time to abandon any remaining fantasies and accept the fact that you are an adoptive parent with an adopted child. You may not have given birth, but you are a true parent.

As you remain focused on the realities of being a true parent, keep in mind that all true parent-child relationships are founded on:

EMOTIONAL AND PSYCHOLOGICAL BONDS.

You have already achieved that.

Now that you are back in reality again, let us consider another aspect of adoption during this stage of your child's development.

Your Children's Questions About Adoption

As your youngsters become more curious about life and birth, they will be more interested in how they fit into the scheme of being. They will already know, from the story you have told them, that they were born and then you adopted them. The inquiring attitude of most preschoolers leads them to wonder how their birth actually came about. If they see a pregnant woman, they may begin to ask some questions:

"Why is that lady so fat?" or
"Why is her stomach sticking out?" or
"What is that lady carrying under her dress?"

Consider these questions as opportunities for you to tell them more about adoption. Sometimes the pregnant woman will be a close friend, a relative, or someone you pass in a shopping mall. You may answer any of their questions by telling your children that the lady is pregnant, which means that she is growing a baby in a special part of her stomach, and when the baby is ready, it will be born.

Your youngsters may be satisfied with your answer and not ask any more questions at that time; however, later on they will probably want to know more. If the pregnant woman is a family member or a friend, they will be more aware of the actual birth and will have additional questions:

"How did the baby come out?"
"Was I born that way?"
"Was I in your tummy, mommy?"
"Why didn't I grow in your tummy?"

The above questions are very typical of those asked by all toddlers, and your children will be no exception. You can be prepared for them by knowing that they will occur and by being as matter-of-fact as possible when you answer them. Tell your children that the baby came out of a special opening that all women have, and that all babies are born that way. Of course, you should tell them that they did not grow in your tummy, but add that they grew in another lady's tummy and then, when they were born, you adopted them. Always tell your children that you are so happy that they were born and are part of your family.

When your children ask why they didn't grow in your tummy, you may answer by telling them that you tried and could not grow babies in your tummy. If you wish, add that you wanted to have a child so they grew in another lady's tummy, and when they were born, you adopted them.

If Daddy is asked these questions about Mommy, he can answer in much the same way. It doesn't matter which parent is infertile; the answers will still suffice. Remember that you are talking to a child—two to five years old—whose understanding is limited. Do not attempt to tell your children more than they can handle. As they get older, you will add more age-appropriate information; we will discuss this process in later chapters.

To summarize, when your toddler questions you about birth and adoption:

- Expect to be questioned.
- Consider it an opportunity.
- Be matter-of-fact when you answer.
- Only answer what you are asked; don't elaborate.

Some children will not be as verbal as others. They may not ask many questions about adoption or other parts of their lives. If your children ask few questions, you may want to look for situations when you can talk about adoption. You will have to be open for the right moment to share the information. Many parents who are not asked about adoption believe that they have been saved from having to talk about it, but it is not going to go away. Even if your children do not say anything about adoption, it does not mean they are not thinking about it. ALL ADOPTEES THINK ABOUT ADOPTION THROUGHOUT THEIR LIVES. IT IS PART OF WHO THEY ARE.

As adoptive parents, you have a responsibility to help your children learn to verbalize their feelings about adoption and to let them know that it is safe to talk to you about it.

The Other Lady

Whenever you discuss adoption with your toddlers, you will probably begin by including the concept of "the other lady." Your children may wonder about her, and, as they get older, they will begin to fantasize about that lady, about what she looked like and what she was like.

Ultimately, your children will know that the other lady was their biomother and that they have a biofather. During this stage of development, however, it is very important not to confuse your youngsters with the idea that they might have another set of parents. Your toddlers are at the very foundation of forming an identity, and in order to develop a strong sense of who they are, they must have only one set of parents. The couple who conceived them should be referred to as "a lady and a man"— ambiguous people with no identity. As your children get older, you may choose to tell them more about their bioparents.

The preschooler may begin to ask more probing questions, especially about the "other lady." You could be asked:

"What did she look like?"
"What was she like?"
"Did you know or meet her?"

If you did not meet her, a possible answer would be "She probably looked very much like you." If you had met her, some possible answers would be:

"She looked a lot like you."
"She was very much like you."
"I did not know her, but I met her."

Occasionally children will ask questions about the "other man," but these questions are rare at this age, and they can be answered in much the same way as those about the "other lady." It is also uncommon to hear toddlers ask "why" they were adopted or relinquished. These questions will be discussed in later chapters.

As your children become more involved with learning about themselves and their adoption, you will also become engrossed in the process. What you thought you might be able to avoid is very much a part of your lives and always will be. With each question, you are forced to look at your own thoughts and feelings about adoption.

Infertility Recheck

During the toddler years and in the future, you will probably be required to talk more about adoption than ever before. For many of you, this may be a time to take out the Infertility Checklist (on page 17) and see where you stand. Carefully tune into your feelings about adoption to determine your comfort level. How comfortable are you during the dialogue with your child? Are you relaxed or tense? Sure or hesitant?

You are setting the climate for open communication. No matter what you say, your emotions will be picked up by your child. You may have all the correct answers, but your child will "hear" your feelings as well as your words, and your emotional state will have the greater impact.

To rid yourself of your infertility baggage:

• Tune into your feelings.
• Know what precipitates your feelings.
• Talk to your spouse about your feelings.
• Review the Infertility Checklist (pages 17–18).
• Keep in mind that you are your child's true parent.

Questions from Others About Adoption

Other people will continue to ask questions about you, your children, and adoption. As your preschoolers' identities emerge, it will become evident that they are (and will continue to be) different from you. Others will notice most the dissimilarities in appearance. Your preschoolers, too, will gradually become aware of the lack of resemblance. Each time you are confronted by others, you will need to determine what you are obligated to answer and what you choose to reply. Many people can be intrusive and irritating, and you may become frustrated and angry each time someone asks a probing question.

Most of the comments you will face at this stage of your children's development will be reminders that you and your youngsters do not look alike. Once you accept the concept that your adopted children are different from you, it will be easier for you to deal with the queries. Be matter-of-fact about the idea that you and your children are not a bit alike and that you do not have to justify that fact to anyone.

People who don't know you may say:

"I can't believe that he's your child."
"Were you like that when you were his age?"
"Does she resemble your husband? She certainly doesn't look like you."
"Do you or your wife wear glasses, too?"
"It doesn't seem as if she's following in your footsteps at all."

People who know you may say:

"I can't believe how different she is from you!"
"His true nature is really coming out."
"How will you be able to handle such an active child? You were never like that."
"Is that what her *real* mother was like?"

Whenever you choose to answer these comments or questions, always assume that they are compliments. Beam with pride and smile affectionately at your child and do not directly answer the question. That will probably be enough in most cases. Always let your youngsters know that you are proud of who they are and what they look like. Do not let anyone intimidate you into saying anything you do not want to say.

Each of you will find a response mode that will work for you.

Adopting a Toddler

Children who are between two and five years old when they are adopted bring with them a whole host of experiences and memories. Their adjustment to a new family will depend a great deal on past relationships. Generally speaking, the older the toddler is, the more difficult the adjustment will be.

Factors other than age will also affect how your children adapt to their new home. For example, they might have lived with only one or with both bioparents prior to placement. They will experience a mourning phase as they grieve about the separation and loss. They had developed a great amount of trust in the original relationship; trusting you and a new family will take time.

Often toddlers will have experienced several living arrangements prior to adoption. They could have been in foster care for several years or shifted from foster care to living with the bioparents, delaying placement for adoption until the preschool years.

If your youngsters have not had a stable environment in early life, they will have a hard time forming close, trusting relationships. Usually they will demonstrate anger at their condition, and it will take some time before they feel secure with their new family.

Expect a difficult adjustment period when you adopt children in this age group or older. There will be times when you are discouraged in your role as parents. If your children continue to have problems adapting to their new home, or if you feel particularly frustrated by the situation, consider seeking counseling from a professional who would be able to offer guidance. An adoptive parent group could also lend support.

In many cases, your youngsters may have come from an abusive or neglectful environment. You may believe that you have saved them from a terrible existence and that they should be grateful to you. When they are not appreciative, you may become angry and resentful. Consider that their behavior is often grounded in fear and, in some cases, even terror. They have been taken away from their caregivers and feel abandoned and rejected. Some children will view themselves as responsible and believe that they are "bad." Your good intentions may not be enough. Your youngsters do not know you and need to build trust. Be consistent and caring; create a solid structure and wait. Over time, they should begin to trust you and accept you into their lives.

Susie and Jim adopted Anne when she was five years old. Anne had been in a different living arrangement every year since she was born. Her biomother had tried to take care of her and would do so whenever she was able to. At other times, Anne was in foster homes—four in all. Finally, when Anne's biomother realized that she could not give Anne the quality care she needed, she relinquished her daughter for adoption.

When Anne arrived in Susie and Jim's home, she was an angry, hostile child with poor language skills who exhibited a great deal of acting-out behavior. She seemed determined to hurt Susie and Jim for what had been done to her. Each night she awakened after having a nightmare. Susie and Jim would find her cowering in the far corner of her bed, clutching at a worn blanket, one of the few items remaining from her past. Nothing could reassure her.

When Susie and Jim brought Anne to my office, she was an angry and scared little girl. Anne was gradually able to work her feelings out through play therapy and sessions with Susie and Jim. After many months, she tentatively accepted them. Although she would continually test them, she came to realize that they would always be there for her. Her past would always be a part of who she was, but she was learning to accept that and move on.

It was not an easy task for Susie, Jim, and Anne to learn how to relate to one another, but they were able to make it happen. Susie and Jim created a structure and foundation for Anne, and Anne learned to understand more about her feelings. There were times when Susie and Jim wanted to give up, but somehow they managed to hang on. Anne is eight years old now, and although she still has angry feelings from the past, she is able to talk to her parents about them. Once she began to feel more at ease in her family, she started to catch up developmentally and is now working at her grade level in her classes.

Not everyone will deal with the problems that Susie and Jim had. Yet, as adoptive parents of preschoolers, you will have some trying moments. The continuous questing behavior of the typical toddler can tire even the most fit parents. With an insatiable curiosity as a motivating force, children of this age group appear to be aware of no limits.

As your children attempt to make sense of the world and themselves, you, their parents, represent stability and reassurance. As wise teachers, you help them to decode and understand all that they are absorbing. You are the foundation and structure that allows your child to move on and grow with confidence.

5

School Days, School Days...

Most children begin kindergarten with a sense of excitement and eagerness, as if they were embarking on a new adventure. Their journey through the school years starts out with both daring and apprehension; they know that they are able to do a great deal without the help of their parents, and yet they are afraid to leave the nurturing environment. Will they succeed? What do they need to know?

As parents you, too, will experience different feelings and thoughts when you send your children off to their first few days of school. They seem so young, so naive. You may wonder if you taught them how to begin to cope in the world or if they have learned enough. You want to protect and encourage them, and, at the same time, you are very proud of who they are becoming and want the world to see and appreciate their talents.

During the next few years, you will watch your youngsters and see their very own personalities emerge. As you realistically set goals together, you and your children will reach an understanding about abilities and limitations. There will be success and failure, joy and pain, ease and difficulty, as your children continue to strive, learn, and perform in the world.

At times it will be a struggle to step back and let your children make mistakes, knowing that they must learn on their own. It will be difficult not to show your disappointment when the goals you set are not realized. At other times, you will soar with pride at unexpected accomplishments. These are years of continuous discovery, as your children further develop their images of themselves.

Leaving the Safety of Home

The early school years are the beginning of an autonomy that your youngsters have never felt before. You will watch in awe and sometimes anxiety as they experiment and test their new-found power. They have become productive, social beings, accomplishing tasks as separate individuals. They will no longer need to rely entirely on you to function in the world.

As your son or daughter grows older and enters school, you may feel a sense of abandonment. This is a time of separation for both of you. You are no longer the absolute authority, and you may not have all of the answers. As you let go, it should be with a measure of trust that your children will be able to take some responsibility for their own well-being. After all, they have already learned a great deal from you. Now it is time to start letting go.

You will see how outside influences affect your youngsters' attitudes and values, and, as all parents, whether biological or adoptive, you may worry since you are no longer able to protect them from exposure to the world around them. They will begin to form their own views, which may be different from yours. As they develop friendships and join social groups at school, they will form opinions that will not necessarily be influenced by you. Their dependence on peer relationships will become more evident as they get older.

Separation Anxiety

You and your children may experience some anxiety when schooling begins. These feelings are based in a fear of the unknown. Once your youngsters find that school can be a safe place, they will be more secure. As they meet new friends and accomplish tasks, they will start believing in themselves and feel comfortable when they are away from you.

You may continue to be anxious, however. Your day may be interrupted by worry about your children, and you may not be at ease when they are not with you.

Some adoptive parents have a hard time sharing their children with anyone else. When they are able to understand their feelings about separation, they usually find that they are afraid they might lose the child they had waited so long for. They cannot bear to consider a time when their child will not be with them.

If you are one of these parents, your feelings can be very real and frightening to you. They may also arouse undue concern for your children. Your children will tune into your feelings because they are so aware of you and your emotions. It will confuse them to hear the unspoken message that you are afraid, and they will wonder why you do not trust them and their competence.

Help yourself and your child by taking the following five steps:

1. Thoroughly explore and understand your feelings about this daily separation.
2. Know that school is a safe environment.
3. Realize that you cannot remain together forever.
4. Participate in activities that you enjoy, to pass the day quickly.
5. Plan for the inevitable separation that will take place when your child becomes an adult.

Styles of Individuality

Your children emerge as individuals during their school years. In this process of continuous discovery, you will watch them become separate persons who accomplish tasks and solve problems. During this time of learning, they will move ahead at their own speed. Each step is based on readiness, and each child has his or her own developmental timetable. As they learn in school, they develop understanding: how to approach a problem and ultimately solve it. You will witness the formation of an individual developing styles and habits that will continue throughout his or her life.

These school years will remind you again of how different your child is from you, although you still may not be ready to relate to, understand, or accept these differences. All parents must confront and deal with dissimilarities among themselves and their children. The school years force parents to look at their sons and daughters more realistically.

As an adoptive parent, you had always believed that you would be able to deal with any disparities between you and your children, but you may not be emotionally prepared. The youngsters you have loved, nurtured, and cared for over the years are becoming the persons they were predisposed to be. They may not be ready to read when you did; they may excel in sports and not science; they may struggle with math; they may love to draw pictures or write poetry; they may be shy or aggressive, quiet or outgoing.

YOUR CHILD WILL BE DIFFERENT FROM YOU.

Learning Abilities

You are watching the formation of an individual. All children show both their abilities and limitations, and before you can help them accept who they are you must be open to knowing your son or daughter.

To help your child learn:

•BE OPEN TO DIFFERENCES BETWEEN YOU AND YOUR CHILD.
At times there will be striking disparities. Occasionally they will be moderate.
•BE OPEN TO LEARNING ABOUT WHO YOUR CHILD IS BECOMING.
Stay aware, informed, tuned in.
•BE OPEN TO ACCEPTING YOUR CHILD AND WHO HE OR SHE IS.
Accepting your child does not mean accepting inappropriate behavior. Chapter 8 discusses setting limits and discipline.

Coping with Learning Disabilities

As you get to know your child, you will discover a person with many assets and probably some limitations. In an effort to help, don't focus on only their disabilities. Any child will see this as disapproval and feel discouraged. If your child has specific learning disabilities, special programs, tutoring, and remediation can minimize, and in some cases eliminate, them. Be open to your child's teacher and the school's assessment of what is needed. Get an independent appraisal as well, and then follow the recommendations.

You may have difficulty accepting the fact that your child has learning disabilities. You may feel a deep sense of responsibility for the problem and assume that you have somehow failed. You haven't. Don't agonize over the situation, because this will send silent messages to your child that you are hurting because of him. Don't burden your child with this responsibility, too.

You may even be angry at your youngster for having these limitations, seeing her performance as a reflection on you. The fact that your child needs special help may embarrass you. Your son or daughter will receive these messages, too, and will feel deeply hurt and helpless about the predicament. In turn, he or she may act out angry feelings toward you.

Your child's learning disability may remind you that he is not perfect, which may, in turn, feed your own feelings of imperfection. As an adoptive parent, you may want to continuously prove to the world that you made the right decision in adopting a child. You may also want to undo your own feelings of inadequacy about your infertility by expecting your child to be faultless.

- Take the time to explore your own feelings.
- Understand your motivations.
- Believe in yourself and in your child.
- Know that no one is at fault.

Success and Self-Worth

Now that you have accepted your family again, let us look at your child's assets and how they can be encouraged. For the most part, children feel good about themselves when their environment is supportive and assuring. If you are overly critical of them, you will find that they will feel defeated and unable to accomplish a task. They will internalize your criticism as a negative force and could lose hope rather than strive further.

As your children grow, you will find that you are not the only ones affecting their success in school. All children are influenced by the competence and enthusiasm of teachers as well as by friends. Your children have their own feelings about their proficiency and self-worth but may become extremely critical of themselves, even when you are most supportive. As they are exposed to the world, they will be more aware of other people's accomplishments. Their friends will serve as examples for them, and they will observe that some of their friends are more capable than they are and may begin to question their own capacities and abilities.

Quite often, youngsters grow according to their own developmental timetable. They may reach a readiness for particular tasks earlier or later than do other children. A child knows that he or she is in the highest or lowest math or reading group, even when not labeled that way.

We know, as adults, that successes in life are usually based on a totality of accomplishments, and we can cite many famous people who had difficulties in their early school years. Children do not have that wider vision, and they are able to focus on only what they are currently experiencing.

All children have their own talents and special abilities, and your child is no exception. Here are ten ways to help your children accept and feel good about themselves in spite of their limitations:

1. Come to terms with their limitations.
2. Help them find their own specialness.
3. Accept their aptitudes.
4. Know that your children's abilities will most likely be different from your own.
5. Appraise successes in terms of their own capabilities and limitations.
6. Support and praise all achievements, no matter how small.
7. Help your children deal with feelings about any limitations by listening.
8. Encourage your children to accept liabilities and be proud of any accomplishments and innate abilities.

9. Get tutorial or remedial help as soon as you are aware of the need.
10. Understand that you can listen and validate your children's feelings, but you may not be able to "make it better."

When we accept our children for who they are, they will feel the freedom to be themselves. Their special capacities will then burst forth.

Adoption Has a Deeper Meaning

Leaving the safety of home has many implications for both the adopted child and the family. As your children step out of your protective and nurturing environment, they will become aware of the world's view of adoption. Until now, you and they have believed that adoption is something warm and special and wonderful. Unfortunately, the rest of the world may not always agree. As a result, during the school years, the adoptive family faces many new issues.

Most people do not have an understanding of adoption and what it means to an adoptive family. They may inadvertently make comments that are hurtful and may misinform their own children about adoption. Adopted children may become hurt and confused by the remarks of their friends.

Frequently, children will come home with questions about comments they have heard at school. One adopted child was told by her friend that she was just like a Cabbage Patch doll, who was an orphan until she was adopted. When she came home from school that day she asked, "Am I an orphan, and what is an orphan, anyway?" Her parents explained to her that an orphan was someone who didn't have a mother or a father and, since she had both, she couldn't be an orphan.

Danny's story is different:

"I hate it! I don't want to be adopted." Laura held her arms out to her six-year-old son and consoled him as he sobbed. Finally, when he was a little quieter, they could talk.

"Now, tell me what happened."

"You said it was special to be adopted. No one else in my class is adopted. I want to be like the other kids!"

As she asked questions, Laura pieced together the story.

During "show-and-tell" time, the children were taking turns standing in front of the class to tell something that was important to them. When Danny's turn came, he said, proudly, "I'm adopted."

The teacher smiled. "Thank you, Danny," she said.

None of the children said anything.

After school, Danny saw several of his classmates waiting outside. One boy called out, "Did all you kids know Danny was adopted?"

That started it. As he passed them, they began chanting, "Dan-ny is a-dop-ted, Dan-ny is a-dop-ted . . ."

"It is special to be adopted," reassured his mother. "They just don't know because they weren't adopted." She gave him a hug.

Laura's heart ached as she thought of the pain her six-year-old had known and might know again.

Both of these children experienced situations common to many adoptees. During the early school years, adopted children will often feel that they are different from their classmates, even if there are several adopted children in a class. They may not be able to understand completely how they are different, but they will know that it is linked to their adoption.

Although your children may not have exactly the same experiences as the ones mentioned above, they will have similar ones that will remind them of being adopted. They will also consider adoption and the meaning of it in a new way as they observe other children who are not adopted.

You will feel helpless and worry about your child, as Laura did. It will not always be easy to deal with your feelings of inadequacy as you are confronted with problems that may have few solutions. This is a critical time for communication between you and your youngster. Be open to listening and understanding, so that your child feels safe to talk about his innermost doubts, fears, and pleasures. It is very difficult for any child to experience a problem at school and not be able to talk about it at home.

Your children want to know that they can talk to you. Allow them to express themselves without judgment or recourse. You can be open to listening without having to necessarily solve the dilemma.

You, too, can be open to expressing your feelings and thoughts on adoption. This openness helps your child understand more about emotions. Show your child that you, too, are human.

As children get older, they want to know more about adoption and what it means to them. If you are comfortable about answering questions and discussing adoption with them, then they will be free to communicate and discuss the issues with you. Each conversation will pave the way to the next and will add to their knowledge of themselves and you. Many adult adoptees say that they always knew that they were adopted, but could not always talk to their parents about adoption because it made their parents uncomfortable. Do not let your children grow up with those feelings. Let them express all of their emotions and be open to listening. You may not have all of the answers, but you can still hear what they have to say.

Adoption Talk

Your children's questions about adoption will take several forms and will fall into some general topics.

Facts About Your Child's Own Adoption

All school-age adopted children are curious and want more information. In an attempt to better understand themselves, they usually want to know more about their bioparents and why they were adopted.

Be ready for these questions:

"Why did she put me up for adoption?"
"Why couldn't she keep me?"
"What was she/he like?"
"Did you know them, meet them?"

You may answer:

"She placed you for adoption because she loved you, but she
   knew that she could not take care of you the way she would
   have wanted."
"She could not keep you because . . ." (Tell your child what
   you know.)
"She/he must have been very much like you" or "They were
   very much like you."
"I never met them" or "I met them when you were born" or
   "I met them before you were born." (Tell your child the
   truth.)

When you answer your children's questions, only give answers for what you have been asked. Eliminate any details that
you believe they are not ready to handle. You will be able to add
more information in time.

How a Child Copes with the Facts
Children are not always able to put the feelings they have into
words. They will show them in many ways. As parents, you will
have to decipher the real meaning so that you can then offer
comfort and support.
   What happens if your child:

EXPRESSES ANGER ABOUT WHAT YOU HAVE SAID?
Support the angry feelings by accepting and validating them.
Tell him that you understand.
COMMUNICATES DISBELIEF ABOUT WHAT HAS BEEN SAID?
Assure your child that what you are saying is the truth and
that you can understand why it is so difficult to accept the
information.

ATTEMPTS TO DISCREDIT THE BIOFAMILY IN ORDER TO FEEL
GOOD ABOUT HERSELF?

In doing so, your child may tell you that the bioparents were
bad people and that is why they placed her for adoption.

Assure your child that her bioparents were good people who
had no other choice.

IS CONFUSED OR DENIES HAVING ANY FEELINGS?

Help your child understand by assuring him that it is appropriate to have feelings about the facts. Suggest that it is hard to
sort out those feelings, and that you are there to help. Then
wait.

If he does not reach out to you, offer additional support.
Eventually he will turn to you, if he knows that you are open to
listening.

HAS FEELINGS IN CONFLICT ABOUT COMMENTS FROM OTHERS?

Your child will always have feelings about comments from
others about adoption. You can help by letting her know that
it is likely that she will have some feelings.

If there is denial, suggest the possibilities—then wait.

You may be relieved when your children are unwilling to
express any sentiments to you, but you must help them get in
touch with their feelings in order to help them work through
those sentiments. If your children are consciously aware of their
deepest feelings, they will be better able to cope with their
adoption. You are the only person with whom they can have an
honest communication. As adoptive parents, you are the only
ones who really understand. At first, it may be very difficult for
you to broach the topic, but be assured that you will be creating
a safe environment in which your children can explore the most
difficult of issues. Even if these issues are closed, keep the ave-
nues of communication about adoption open.

Adopting the School-Age Child

Couples who adopt children five to eleven years old will deal
with many significant issues. These children have a multitude of
experiences and memories. They may have lived with their bio-

parents before being placed for adoption because of the death of one or both of them or a change of circumstances. A grandparent or other family member may have been the primary caregiver. Many children of this age group have spent time in different foster homes, never being able to maintain any steady relationships.

Whatever the circumstances prior to the adoption, these children will probably be in a state of mourning for some time. Having experienced one or a number of losses, they will need to grieve in order to find a safe and comfortable place with you. You will also encounter anger, which may be profound, so expect resistance to any new attachments. Anger at this age and in this situation may take several forms: withdrawal; apathetic or sullen moods, possibly deep depression; wanting to run away; hostility and aggression toward oneself, others, and/or property.

Much of the outrage and acting-out will be directed at you, the new parents, so seriously consider getting some counseling support during these first months and at the first sign of abnormal behavior. It will help ease the burden of parenting and allow you to accept one another and the new situation by getting off on the right foot.

This anger stems from feelings of inadequacy and low self-esteem. These children believe that they must have been "bad" or their bioparents would not have abandoned them. In an attempt to punish these rejecting parents, the child makes the adoptive parents the scapegoats. Quite often, with therapy, many of the problems can be worked through. Occasionally, even therapy will be of minimal benefit and only time and patience will help.

Once you put all of the issues of these developmental years to rest, you can move into the stages of puberty and adolescence with more confidence. You and your child can proceed in a joint collaboration of love and respect.

6

Another Child Arrives

As you anticipate the arrival of another child, you will have mixed feelings of excitement and joy about the upcoming event and concerns about the added responsibility of caring for one more human being. Some old doubts and fears may emerge. You will wonder if you can handle one more child, what the child will be like, and how your youngster will accept and deal with a new sibling.

All parents can relate to these emotions and conflicting thoughts. As adoptive parents, you will discover additional sensitivities about adding to your family. At times there will be reminders of the emptiness you felt when you were childless and of the uncertainties that accompanied the wait for your first child. You may worry about experiencing all of the emotional pain again.

Then you will rekindle the memories of what it was like when you first became a family, and those warm, comfortable thoughts will spur you on to have another child. As you prepare for the exciting event, it is important to consider what the arrival of another child means to your adoptive family.

Most adopted children believe that they have a special relationship with their parents. As adoptive parents, you always tell them how significant their adoption is. Through your stories and dialogue you show them how much they mean to you. Now your youngsters have to accept another special person in your life.

54

All families experience many adjustments when a new child arrives. The older children must learn how to compromise and share their parents, and the parents must make room for another child who also has needs that must be met. Parents must share love, time, and energy with all of the children and still have room for themselves, as individuals and as a couple. It's not an easy feat.

When a child comes into an adoptive family, parents and children may be more sensitive to the adjustments. Adoptive families are more susceptible to strong feelings about the arrival of a new child. Like all children, adopted children feel insecure and displaced by a new brother or sister. Their parents may feel guilty about wanting another child and will try to protect their older children from the impact of the event. The guilt is usually connected to their need to protect their children from reexperiencing any feelings of the original abandonment by their biomothers. They believe that wanting another child is a betrayal of their love for their older children.

Adopted children do have strong feelings about the arrival of a sibling. Some may even feel responsible for their parents' need to adopt another child, as if they have failed in some way. They may wonder how they can be so special if their parents want someone else, and they may become angry or sullen, or they may be overeager to please their parents in an effort to win back their love.

When you see your children's reactions to the prospect of a sibling, you may experience more guilt and try to deny your needs, deciding never to have another child, or you may become oversolicitous of your children in an attempt to prove your love. In either case, you are not confronting the real issue: You want your family to grow.

Let's face it. You are an adoptive family. You can't change that fact. With adoption come feelings and emotions that cannot be denied and must be dealt with each step of the way.

Now that you are ready to accept your role again, let's look at how you can plan for and create a welcoming atmosphere for another special child.

Preparing Your Child for a New Sibling

You can allay your child's concerns about having a brother or sister by helping him to understand what it will be like. When your child has some information, he will be better able to make the necessary adjustments. Take the following steps before the new child arrives.

Tell your youngsters:

WHAT BABIES ARE LIKE.
Describe in detail how babies cry, sleep, eat, and behave.
If you are adopting an older child, characterize that child's behavior.

Explain:

WHAT YOUR RELATIONSHIP WITH THE NEW CHILD WILL BE LIKE.
Give your child information about a typical day and how you will spend your time with the new child.

Discuss:

WHAT YOUR CHILD'S RELATIONSHIP WITH A BROTHER OR SISTER WILL BE LIKE.

Talk about:

WHAT YOUR RELATIONSHIP WITH BOTH OF YOUR CHILDREN WILL BE LIKE.
Let your child know how much you love and care for him or her. Discuss your limitations, how you will have to share your time and your love. Talk specifically about how this will happen.

Explore:

WHAT YOUR CHILD FEELS OR WANTS AND WHAT HE OR SHE WOULD LIKE.

Talk about possible jealousy, anger, and sadness.

Be honest and direct. Your child will have these feelings, and it is important for him or her to know that you understand.

Clarify:

WHAT YOUR CHILD'S NEW POSITION IN THE FAMILY WILL BE LIKE. Define new responsibilities and privileges. Help your child feel the specialness of being the older (or younger) sibling.

Getting your child ready for the upcoming event will assist you in planning ahead. As you prepare, you will be looking for ways to involve your child in the process. She can help you get the room ready, select clothing, sort through toys, or rearrange furniture.

No matter how much you tell your child, however, and how prepared she is, she will still have some powerful feelings about having a brother or sister. The preparation is important because it helps to set the scene for open dialogue and allow for continued communication. Your child will feel more safe in expressing any emotions or thoughts, and you will be able to continue to talk more freely with her.

As you prepare your family for the arrival of a new child, let's consider what is involved for all of you. Whether you expect an adopted or biological child, you can anticipate some predictable events. Your children will:

• Feel insecure and displaced.
• Perceive the new child as an intruder.
• Believe that they are loved less or not enough.
• Fear you will abandon them.
• Want the brother or sister to go away.

All children have these feelings and thoughts, but they are more profound for adopted children because they believe that if they were abandoned once, then it could happen again. You can reassure your adopted children, but you cannot make their feelings go away.

After your new child arrives, your older youngsters may

change their behavior or act out in order to get your attention. They may regress and attempt to drink from the baby's bottle or want one of their own. If they have already been toilet trained, they may wet or soil in order to force you to be more involved with them. These behaviors should last only a short time, and as your older children begin to feel secure again, they will resume their usual routines.

Your school-age children will probably be more vocal about their objections to the new child. They will express anger (at times, outrage) about the event. Gradually they will learn to accommodate. Accepting their feelings as normal and allowing them to talk to you about them will make the situation easier for all of you.

As parents, you will also go through adjustments with the arrival of another child. You and your spouse will:

- Reexperience your feelings about your infertility.
- Doubt your capacity to parent another child.
- Attempt to accommodate the needs of one more family member.
- Rebalance your relationship.
- Realize your great capacity for loving.

Your experiences will be very much like those of other families, but as adoptive parents you may have more concerns about your roles. You've done it before, but you may wonder if you can do it again. You may have initial doubts, but after your new child arrives, you will realize that you have what it takes to be the parents you want to be.

Family and friends will also be involved with each new child. Your family and friends will:

- Anticipate your new child with excitement.
- Share in the joy of the occasion.
- Make comments about your children.
- Ask further questions about adoption.

Once again, you will be placed in the position of listening to comments and answering questions about adoption. You will find that the questions will be similar to those asked when you adopted your first child. The arrival of a biological child may cause additional remarks. For example, one inquisitive neighbor wanted to know if a couple loved their biological child more than their adopted one. Of course, all parents know that their love is for all of their children and cannot be measured.

The Adopted Sibling

When you adopt other children, you have the opportunity to reinforce your feelings and attitudes about adoption. With each new child, a stronger sense of family develops, and a bond of mutuality strengthens among the children. They all have something in common with one another and are connected to you in a similar way.

You can now repeat your children's adoption stories, and they will be able to experience firsthand what it was like when they were adopted. They will see how excited you are and connect this delight with how you felt about their own adoption. They, too, can share in the excitement.

Your children can not only help you plan for the arrival of another child but also be there for the event. Their participation will help them feel closer to you and relate to what it was like when they were adopted. You may have your children go to the hospital or to the lawyer's, doctor's, or agency office to bring their brother or sister home. They will be overjoyed at the prospect of being included in this momentous occasion.

After you bring your new child home and family and friends visit, continue to make your older children part of the celebration. Let them help you show off the new child. After all, they now have an important position in the family—older brother or sister. Tell everyone how significant their roles really are. Glow with pride at your older children's notable characteristics: They still have unique abilities worthy of mention and praise.

Your first adopted child can also be part of the occasion when an older child is adopted. Let your first child help his new brother or sister become acclimated. He may make the introductions to family members and he can be a general source of information for the new child. Your new child will feel allied with the younger sibling and a bond of attachment between the siblings will begin to form.

The Biological Sibling

When a biological child joins an adoptive family, there are additional issues to deal with. Certainly the preparations will be the same, and your children can participate fully in the upcoming arrival. Their assistance and support will probably be most welcome.

Conceiving and bearing a child will evoke many old feelings for you as parents as well as create new emotions. You will be in conflict about many of them. Suddenly you have the biological child that you had wished for, the one that you had mourned and accepted you would never have. You will feel an enormous love for your adopted children and may believe that you have somehow betrayed them by giving birth to a child.

Your adopted children will also be confused about their feelings. Depending on their age, they will have many mixed emotions. They might be jealous and angry about the fact that they were not born to you and will have a greater sense of being different. At times, they will display rivalry, create conflicts, and show jealousy toward their brothers and sisters. All children experience sibling rivalry, but when there are both adopted and biological children in a family, there can be great competition among them.

As adoptive parents, you will want to make it all better. It is difficult to watch your children hurt, and you will feel helpless. You will want to help all your children, whether adopted or biological, work through their feelings about one another. Your children need to know that there are different ways to have a family and that you love all of them very much. This will be an easy thing for you to say because you believe it to be so.

Biological siblings will also have feelings about their position in the family and must have opportunities to talk about these feelings with you. Often they carry a burden of guilt about being the biological child and may harbor other sensitivities. Biological children in an adoptive family may feel so guilty that they will want to make it up to their adopted siblings by offering them prized possessions or, in some cases, by taking responsibility for punishable acts that their adopted brothers or sisters actually committed. These biological children seem to feel a need to apologize to their siblings for being born into the family and not adopted.

Other biological siblings may assume the role of entitled heir and try to push their weight around in the family. They will attempt to impose themselves on their adopted siblings and continuously remind them of their differences. These children can create serious problems within the family unless this behavior is stopped. They may extend their beliefs outside the family and find strong opposition.

In other families, the adopted siblings may try to bully the biological ones. In one family, the adopted children called the biological child the "oddball." Name-calling and abuse can have serious affects on children and must be stopped immediately by the parents.

Sibling Rivalry

Feelings of jealousy and competition are common among siblings in all families. Often, the conflicts are between children who are close in age, but rivalry may also occur between children years apart.

Occasionally brothers and sisters will carry their intense feelings into adulthood, particularly when they have forceful personalities and strong feelings of entitlement in the family. Quite often this rivalry occurs despite the parents' efforts to discourage it.

Adoptive parents may inadvertently support their children's conflicts by not setting appropriate limits. They may be afraid to take a stand for fear that their children might feel rejection and believe that they are not loved. There may be times when your children will really feel rejected by you and you by them, and no matter what you do, you will not be able to change these feelings.

In other situations, you may attempt to take sides or to mediate disputes. Usually this approach does not work. One child may be blamed for things he did not do, and another may get away without any responsibility. This further reinforces conflicts and they will flare up repeatedly as your children hope that you will take sides. The children will feel a greater sense of challenge each time and will look for opportunities to create arguments.

Parents may also create difficulties by trying to make everything the same for all of their children. They believe that if they strive for equality, they will reduce the possibility of conflict. Instead, the children keep checklists and are quick to tell the parents when brothers and sisters get more than they do. The parents then end up in a never-ending attempt to keep everything even, trying to prove their fairness.

In many families, competitive feelings are reinforced when each child is labeled. We know that all children are different. Some become favorites; others become difficult. When you expect your children to behave in a certain way, they will usually comply, and the difficult child will often become envious of the favored one. Conflicts and tensions are then inevitable.

Here are some guidelines to help you minimize conflicts among your children.

You *should not:*

• ALLOW ANY PHYSICAL ABUSE TO TAKE PLACE BETWEEN YOUR YOUNGSTERS.

You may need to separate them until they are ready to talk to each other about a resolution.

• POINT OUT DIFFERENCES IN A WAY THAT WILL LABEL YOUR CHILDREN OR POKE FUN AT THEM.

Do not give them further ammunition to create conflicts.

• CARRY THE BURDEN OF YOUR CHILDREN'S ACTS.

What they do may embarrass you, but they are the ones who should feel humiliated, not you.

• TRY TO MAKE EVERYTHING THE SAME.

It is impossible to create equality. When you come to terms with this fact, your children will not expect rigid uniformity.

•ANTICIPATE THAT YOUR LOVE WILL BE THE SAME FOR ALL OF YOUR CHILDREN.

Love is not equal, and you will love each child for his or her own self.

You *should:*

•ENCOURAGE YOUR CHILDREN TO SOLVE THEIR OWN DISPUTES.

If they know that they cannot expect you to work out the problems for them, they will try to take care of themselves and assume responsibility for the solutions.

•ACCEPT YOUR CHILDREN'S DIFFERENCES AND TREAT EACH ACCORDING TO INDIVIDUAL NEEDS.

They will believe that they are being treated fairly and will have less of a reason to be jealous of a sibling.

•EXPECT YOUR CHILDREN TO TAKE RESPONSIBILITY FOR THEIR OWN ACTIONS.

If they know that they are all being made accountable, they will have fewer complaints that brothers or sisters are getting away with something.

•BELIEVE THAT YOU CAN MINIMIZE COMPETITION IN YOUR FAMILY BY TREATING YOUR YOUNGSTERS WITH FAIRNESS AND A SENSE OF COURTESY AND RESPECT.

•BE CERTAIN THAT YOUR LOVE IS FOR ALL OF YOUR CHILDREN AND THAT IT WILL ENDURE.

The Only Child

Some of you may choose to have only one child. It is important to consider the unique needs of the family with the only child. Parents of only children do not have the opportunity to observe their child living and playing with other children on a day-to-day basis in their own family. When your perspective is limited, your expectations may be based on unrealistic ideas.

As you focus all of your parenting energy on one child, you may place a greater burden on that child. You may attribute to your youngster many qualities that don't fit and bestow an overabundance of gifts on him or her. Hoping to be the very best parents possible, you may believe that you must show your child how much loving and caring you have. What starts out as involvement and caring often ends up as overindulgence and smothering.

An adopted child who is an only child has more problems to solve when he is showered with affection and rewards. He is faced with a dilemma. Is he being rewarded for himself or for his accomplishments? What if he is unable to meet his parents' expectations? Will he still be loved? Then he starts to rationalize. Of course, he's loved! Look at all he has been given.

When adoptive parents overidealize their children, they create additional difficulties for them. All children carry a sense of entitlement when they are looked at as perfect. At the same time, however, they feel inadequate because they know that no one can really be perfect. These conflicting feelings force these youngsters to assume an inflated self-image, which they then carry into other relationships.

Only children are more prone to these inner tensions because their parents have only one child to focus on. When any child, adopted or biological, is treated preferentially, he or she tends to have poor peer relationships, feeling alone and never fitting in. They usually find fault with their peers who will not treat them as their parents do. Then they turn to their parents for friendship instead of to children their own age.

If you are willing to assume the inappropriate role of "pal" to your children, they will have difficulty understanding the appropriate boundaries between parent and child and become confused about their role in the family. The parent-child relationship should be one in which the parent is the authority; the child looks to the parent for guidance. You are the teacher; your child is the student. When the roles are not clearly defined, your children become confused and insecure.

Adopted children who are only children do not have the benefit of watching you interact with brothers and sisters. All of their information about what parents and children are like comes only from their relationship with you. When the roles are not clearly stated, your son or daughter will become confused and insecure and more perplexed about his or her self-worth and identity.

Children look to their parents for validation of who they are. As you help them draw a realistic picture of themselves, they will be able to abandon any false, inflated images. They need you to help define themselves and others in the world. Your appropriate encouragement and support will allow your child to develop a sense of self-worth as a child and as a person.

7

Adopting a Special-Needs Child

Parents of special-needs children will deal with issues that are more complex than those of other adoptive parents. You have children with special problems and special needs that will require some additional awareness and preparedness. Your family will face all of the adoption-related issues as well as the particular requirements of your special-needs child.

As adoptive parents, you have made a commitment to yourselves and to your children to be the very best parents possible. By knowing a little more about what you will experience, you can help your special-needs children deal with their adoption.

The Older Child

In chapters 3, 4, 5, and 11 we discuss what you and your youngsters will experience when you adopt children who are older than two or three years old. These children will have a more difficult time adjusting to you because they will have memories of the past. Their relationship to you will depend greatly on how well they are able to work through their feelings about former relationships and on how safe they feel with you. They will be more sensitive to issues relating to separation, loss, abandonment, and trust. Building a new trusting relationship will take time and a great deal of patience.

No matter how abusive or negative the former settings were,

these children will not be grateful to you. You may believe that you have saved them from terrible circumstances, but they may not always agree. Their past experiences probably taught them to mistrust and be wary of anyone who comes into their lives. At first they will view you as strangers who may harm them.

These children may harbor rage toward the people who had rejected or abandoned them. Even children whose parents had died will feel anger and will need to mourn the loss of their biological parents. They must take the time to grieve before they can consider you as their parents. Your understanding and support will help them move on.

Youngsters who had lived in various foster homes, orphanages, or sporadically with their bioparents will have the most difficulty in making an adjustment. They may see you as enemies, not caring friends, and may even believe that you have taken them from former caregivers against their will. Your time, patience, and a great deal of understanding will help all of you through these anxious times.

Some children may become confused and think that you are really their bioparents who have come to rescue them. They want to believe that their bioparents really want them, and this fantasy is their way of reconciling the abandonment and rejection they feel. You may be tempted to agree with them; however, these children know at some level of understanding that you in fact are not their bioparents, and if you lie to them they will use that deceit as proof that they cannot trust you.

When you adopt older infants and children be sure that you allow them to bring meaningful items of the past with them—a teddy, a blanket, a doll. Older children may want to have their books and other significant mementos. These possessions help them to bridge the gap and are positive connections to the past that they need to help them deal with their separation from it.

Even older adopted children need information about their biological heritage. It may be difficult for you to tell your children what they need to know because you may have angry feelings about circumstances in their past, but they must have the facts so that they can come to terms with their own identity. They may want to reject what you tell them because of their own emotions, but you must help them handle the important information. Before you share anything with your children, be sure that it is age appropriate. Don't tell them anything that they are not ready to hear.

Be prepared for a great impact on your family when you adopt an older child, whether you have other children or this is your first child. If you find that you are unable to cope with the special problems of the older child, consult a professional counselor. A therapist can help your family make a more stable transition.

The Physically/Emotionally Handicapped Child

If you adopt children who have physical or emotional handicaps, you will feel a greater impact on your family than do other adoptive parents. These children will demand more of your time and energy and will need more attention. When you choose to adopt these children, you make a commitment to parent in a special way.

Many handicapped children are older, so you will also deal with issues related to adopting the older child. Most important for your particular family is that you allow enough time for you and your spouse. Be sure that you spend time together. Get away from your children from time to time to renew your relationship and replenish your energy.

Give your other children the necessary attention. Many children who have a handicapped brother or sister grow up too fast and lose the childhood that is crucial to development because they may have the responsibility of caring for their handicapped sibling or must deal with problems alone because Mom or Dad is overly involved with their handicapped brother or sister. You may have to juggle and balance, but you can give all of your children the attention they need and deserve.

Children from Other Countries

Some of you have adopted children who were born in other countries. In most instances, they came to you as infants, and you are raising them as all adopted children are reared. Begin to use the word *adoption* early and continue to develop your children's own adoption story as they get older. Your values and culture will become their own, and they will be very much a part of the country in which they are raised.

In addition, you should help them learn about both their biological heritage and their culture. Your children should have information about the country from which they came—the people, the culture, any attributes that make that place unique. Bone up on the facts because your youngsters deserve to know as much as possible. As they get older, they may want to do more research on their own. Whatever they learn will help them to establish their own identity. Help them to develop a sense of pride in their heritage.

Biracial and Transracial Children

Those of you who adopt biracial or transracial youngsters will parent children who often will be very different from you in appearance. Like all adoptive families, you will deal with the issues related to adoption. Your children do not resemble you and the unlikeness will be obvious to everyone. As is the case for all adopted children, people may ask you many questions about your children, or, because of the apparent dissimilarities, they may not question you at all. Some people may make the assumption that these children are not really yours and are just visiting for the day.

Many parents of biracial or transracial youngsters tend to be overly protective, believing that they need to shield their children from the misguided comments of others. Some parents are very verbal about the fact that their children are adopted, as if to ward off comments. Treat these special-needs kids as you would any other children who happen to be adopted. The needs of your family are the same as those of all adoptive families.

As parents of biracial and transracial youngsters, you will probably not have to contend with your fantasies that your children could be just like you. The evident unlikeness between you and your children should allow you to create more realistic goals for them and to set appropriate expectations based on who they are and not on who you are. Help them to understand and to preserve their cultural heritage. Their uniqueness can best be understood within the framework of their biological beginnings.

Special-Needs Parents

As adoptive parents of special-needs kids, you will experience adoption in the same way all other adoptive families do. Adoption will be part of your lives, and you will learn to deal with the issues and questions as your children develop and grow into adults. In many ways you will also be like all parents, coping with problems, feeling stressed one day and proud the next, knowing that you are doing what is needed to help your children reach their potential. You will believe in them and in yourself and accept your limitations and theirs: You are real parents with real children.

8

Morals, Manners, Discipline, Values, and All Those Good Things

Most parents feel a profound responsibility to help their children become productive, competent adults. They want to instill morals and values in their youngsters that will be part of them all of their lives. Parents, through their guidance, are preparing their children for life.

When you adopt children, you will also want to teach them what is important to you and what you hold dear. What you expect of your youngsters is usually what society and others expect. How you go about sharing what you value with your children is usually a complex process.

Over the years, parents have been greatly influenced by psychological theory and practice. Those who take their roles seriously may become overburdened and confused by the many messages they receive about child-rearing. All parents have doubts and worry that even their good intentions could actually be harmful.

All parents have concerns about child-rearing. You will want to be the very best parent possible, with children who feel good about themselves and respect the society and culture in which they live.

Before you decide how you will parent, let's look at some of your attributes as parents, and more particularly as adoptive parents.

When You Are a Parent

You Are a Teacher

All parents are teachers and models of behavior. Through your words and actions, you help your children learn what is acceptable so that they become responsible human beings. Your guidance helps them to become the productive, competent adults they deserve to be. Your leadership allows them to understand their culture and the morals and values that society deems important. Your family is a microcosm of society.

You Are Human

Even though you make conscious decisions as a parent not to repeat your own parents' mistakes, you will still face pitfalls, difficult times, and some crises. As you watch your children grow and develop, you will discover that parenting is a challenging job.

Adoptive parents may inadvertently add to the responsibilities of parenting by expecting flawless families with ideal children and no problems. They may believe that they must be perfect parents with perfect children. All parents who anticipate perfect families set themselves up for failure.

If you expect an ideal family, your children will often feel as if they have failed because no one can be perfect. Once you set those expectations, you will fail whenever you and your children make mistakes, just like everyone else.

Always keep in mind:

PERFECTION IS A MYTH.

Fear of failure and anxieties about parenting usually feed into expectations about the ideal family. Many adoptive parents are afraid that they will not be good parents. Their need to be perfect may stem from their feelings of inadequacy about their infertility, or they may believe that they must prove that they are adequate because they have adopted children. They feel that their families are being questioned and judged by others, and they must show the world that they're the very best.

When parents do not feel adequate, they set unrealistic and unattainable goals for themselves and their children, which can create a continuous pattern of disappointment for their families. The failure they were trying to avoid becomes a reality.

Don't fall into the perfection trap. You can be an adequate parent without being perfect. Accept your limitations. You are allowed to make mistakes—after all, you are human.

Adoptive parents who are human:

- Are real.
- Make mistakes.
- Get angry and frustrated.
- Don't have all of the answers.
- Are just like all other parents.

Your Children Are Human

All children make mistakes and yours will be no exception. They behave according to what they have already learned, to their temperament, to age and stage of development, and to their level of emotional and intellectual competence. The possibilities of individual differences are infinite. Children learn about appropriate behavior within the framework of their individuality and needs.

During your youngsters' formative years, you will be setting the groundwork for lifetime patterns. Their actions will be based on both their unique needs and your objectives and goals for them.

Accept your children's limitations. They will make mistakes. They are human, just like you.

Adopted children who are human:

- Are real.
- Make mistakes.
- Get angry and frustrated.
- Don't have all of the answers.
- Are just like all other children.

Goal-Setting

When you consider goals for your youngster's behavior, first look at your long-term expectations and then at the steps to get there. As you observe your children from infancy to adulthood, you will see abilities and limitations changing with each age and stage of development. Your expectations for a twelve-year-old will not be the same as those for his or her five-year-old sibling.

Amy was always telling her seven-year-old son Joey to act his age. She had become frustrated by his behavior and believed that he was deliberately trying to ignore her wishes.

Joey's father, Jim, had given up on trying to be involved with his son and had decided that Joey would never be the son he had always dreamed about. Jim also chastised Amy for ever wanting to adopt a baby and thought that they would have been better off as a childless couple.

When the family first came to see me, they were at their wits' ends and each one was blaming the other.

As we began to explore the problem together, we discovered that both Amy and Jim had little information about the typical seven-year-old, about what to expect and how to help their son. It became very clear that Amy and Jim needed to adjust their goals based on Joey's age-appropriate behavior and individual needs.

When Amy and Jim reconsidered what they were doing, they realized that their inflexibility had created doubts about their competence as parents and Joey's perception of himself. Joey had always felt like a bad boy, and Amy and Jim had believed that they were inadequate parents.

Once Amy and Jim identified the problem, they were able to set realistic goals for their son. They realized how much Joey was their child and how they really loved him. Jim began to spend more time with Joey, and as they got to know each other, a deep respect and caring formed.

When Joey was allowed to act his age, Amy and Jim could appreciate him more.

Many parents can relate to Amy and Jim's experience. In both biological and adoptive families, children don't always act the way their parents would like nor do they grow up to be what their parents planned or expected (see chapter 9, "Nature or Nurture").

Most of you would agree that your long-range primary objective for your children is to help them become responsible, productive, and satisfied adults. To achieve your ultimate expectations, you should consider each stage of development and then set suitable minigoals based on your children's capacities. If you are parents of a very bright youngster, you may tend to focus on his or her intellectual competence and lose sight of the emotional level at which he or she is functioning. Similarly, children who are lagging developmentally in various abilities may be expected to perform tasks beyond their level of maturity. Tune in to your children so that you know what is right for them.

Consider your children's temperaments when you set your plans for them. They may have limited attention spans or prolonged ones, and you will be required to structure the environment accordingly. Some need to have instruction given to them bit by bit; others can absorb large quantities of information. One child may have a highly developed auditory perception and another may be visually superior. Their differences and styles of perceiving the world will affect the way they understand what you tell them. You may need to repeat your message many times for some children and only once for others.

Generally speaking, give simple commands without complicated explanations to toddlers and preschoolers. You can elaborate more with the older child.

Most important is the fact that all of your children are separate individuals and should be treated as such. What works for one will not necessarily work for all. Your children will feel most successful if your goals for them are realistic. With appropriate guidelines from you, they will succeed and believe in their effectiveness. They will feel confident. Then they will strive to achieve what is expected of them and gain a sense of accomplishment. They will want to please you because it feels good.

At times, you may judge your children's behavior against that of other children, or you may compare their actions to what you had done at the same age or in a similar situation. Just remember that your children are individuals. As adoptive parents, you should be able to accept individual differences more easily than most parents. If you attempt to compete with other parents and expect your children to be just like their friends, you will guarantee frustration for both you and your youngsters.

When you set goals for your children's behavior, you can minimize your mistakes and disappointments by following these six steps:

1. Understand their unique needs.
2. Consider their age.
3. Realize their level of developmental maturity.
4. Make adjustments based on their temperaments.
5. Know how they absorb information.
6. Don't compete with your friends and their children.

Your youngsters will accept your direction more readily when you have considered their needs and abilities. They will be better able to internalize your expectations and make them their own.

When you have decided how you want your children to behave and what you need to teach them, you are ready to take action.

Guiding Your Children

Most parents begin to set goals for their children before they have them. Many of you probably have a long list of unacceptable behaviors that you will never allow your son or daughter to display. Some of your friends' youngsters probably behaved in ways that you believe are completely out of line. You may even discuss your disapproval with your spouse and decide that you will never let your child "do *that.*"

Now that you have youngsters and you are ready to decide what's best for your family, you may realize that it is not easy to implement a plan that will work. You know what you don't want to see happen, but it is difficult to find ways to shape your child's behavior into acceptable forms.

Here are some suggestions that may be helpful to you. They are based on a foundation of mutual respect among you, your spouse, and your children.

A Step-by-Step Approach

1. SIT DOWN WITH YOUR SPOUSE AND DETERMINE YOUR ULTI- MATE OBJECTIVES.

Do this ideally when your children are infants; however, it is never too late to start. Talk about your basic philosophies, what you ultimately want for your children and for your family as a whole.

Listen carefully. Share what you have heard. Check it out with your partner. Be clear about your spouse's position.

2. NEGOTIATE.

You may not completely agree. Decide on compromises that will work for both of you.

3. DEVELOP GUIDELINES TO REACH YOUR OBJECTIVES.

These plans will be dynamic. You will make modifications as you get to know your youngster's unique style.

Your own needs may also change and need adjustment.

4. UNDERSTAND ONE ANOTHER'S NEEDS.

Leave room for each person to express what he or she be- lieves is important. Check out your ideas with one another.

Be willing to consider different approaches.

5. NEGOTIATE.

6. LISTEN TO YOUR CHILDREN'S NEEDS.

Your youngsters will tell you a great deal. Be open to making adjustments to fit who they are.

When your children are very young, trust your own intuition. As they get older, they will tell you their needs directly.

Let your children express themselves. Their input is valuable.

7. ESTABLISH CHOICES FOR YOUR CHILDREN.

Build a framework of guidelines with some flexibility. Don't be rigid; don't set unreachable goals.

8. NEGOTIATE.

9. TELL YOUR CHILDREN EXACTLY WHAT YOU EXPECT OF THEM.

Be clear and concise about what you want.

The young child needs direct, brief statements. The older child will tune you out if you get too wordy and begin to lecture.

Talk to your children with your spouse present.

10. CREATE APPROPRIATE CONSEQUENCES AS NEEDED.

Consequences for inappropriate behavior should be natural and logical.

11. REMEMBER THAT YOUR ROLE IS TEACHER, NOT PENALIZER.

Your youngsters are learning new behavior from you. They may need time to absorb it.

Leave room for their mistakes. Guide them; lead them; teach them.

12. ENCOURAGE AND SUPPORT YOUR CHILDREN THROUGH THIS LEARNING PROCESS.

Be positive. Tell them how much you appreciate their efforts. Give them another chance.

Praise them for their successes.

13. BE CONSISTENT AND PREDICTABLE.

Don't surprise your children with new rules.

Discuss any changes or new expectations with them.

14. ALLOW FOR A COOPERATIVE SPIRIT AND EFFORT IN IMPLEMENTING YOUR PLAN.

Encourage an attitude of mutual respect and trust among all family members.

Create times to discuss problems and grievances within the family. Let your children participate in the process.

15. DO NOT BE AFRAID TO TAKE A STAND.

Stick to what you believe in. Know that there are some stands that you can never compromise.

Expect your children to be accountable for their behavior and their mistakes.

16. BE UNIFIED BUT FLEXIBLE.

Know that you can be effective.

Admit when you have made a mistake. Let your children know that you are human.

Once you have worked out a framework for appropriate behavior, you and your children will have a better idea of what is expected. As parents you serve as the foundation for growth, change, and reality-testing for them. When you accept your role and know that you can accomplish your tasks, your children will be able to successfully complete their own.

Single-Parent Families

In recent years, more single adults are adopting children. If you are a single parent, the guidelines listed here should help you, but, of course, you will not have the opportunity to check with a spouse about your ideas and will be setting goals alone. Try joining a support group for adoptive parents: There you will get input from other parents who are working on similar issues. You will not feel so alone in making decisions for your youngsters.

If You Are Divorced

If you adopt children and then divorce, you and your former spouse should still be able to work out goals for your children's behavior. If this is not possible, you can join an adoptive parents support group as you develop a plan and discuss problems as they occur. Other parents may have some useful ideas to help you.

Your former spouse may not deal with issues in the same way as you do; however, your children will learn to adjust to the differences in each household. If you feel secure with your decisions, your children will know that they must follow your direction when they are with you.

Many groups for single parents have been established to offer support and guidance for the parent who is raising a child alone. These groups create an atmosphere for sharing, support, and friendship. Both biological and adoptive single parents can benefit a great deal from these groups. However, adoptive single parents need to have additional input about adoption from other adoptive families.

Your Family's Emotional Well-Being

The emotional climate in your home will affect your children's behavior. Youngsters easily pick up the emotional states of people around them. Quite often they will become anxious if you are afraid or insecure. They will know when you are angry, sad, or upset and may react with erratic behavior.

A stable, permanent relationship with your spouse helps to enhance your family's feelings about one another. You and your spouse will set the example for your children. They will see your relationship as a model for them. Your children will learn to treat you and other people with that same mutual respect and caring.

Behavior problems usually occur in families when parents:

- Are rigid and inflexible in their expectations.
- Physically or verbally abuse their children.
- Withdraw love from their children.
- Are unusually punitive.
- Create power struggles within the family.
- Overindulge their youngsters.

Your children need you. For the most part, they want to please. Their greatest fear is being abandoned, not losing love. All children feel this way, but adopted children are particularly sensitive to abandonment issues, and so are adoptive parents. Don't let your feelings about abandonment interfere with your parenting efforts. When your children act in a negative manner, they may simply be testing their relationship with you and their own identity.

You should not, however, permit your child to physically or verbally abuse you, nor should you abuse your child. Deal with your mutual anger in a reasonable way. Sometimes a "breathing time" is needed before you can talk about your feelings. Statements like "I don't like you, Mommy (or Daddy)" or "I hate you" are usually expressions of their anger. Determine what your children are angry about and help them talk about it.

If you are particularly sensitive, your children will know it and may try to manipulate and punish you by withdrawing their love. They may even tell you that you're not their real parent so they don't have to listen to you. If you believe that *you* are their true parents, even though they may have a set of bioparents, then your children will realize that their statements have no effect on you. Encourage them to talk about their feelings. Help them to validate their perceptions and to understand their emotions.

As you allow your children to give credence to their feelings, they will begin to develop a sense of worth and value as human beings. When you disapprove of their actions, let them know that although you cannot accept their *behavior,* you still accept *them.* Never permit them to perceive themselves as "bad."

Older children will be better able to talk about their emotions. They need to know that you will not attack them when they have feelings and opinions that differ from yours. Let them understand that you respect them, and you are ready to work out mutually satisfying solutions to problems. As they get to know what is best for them, they will struggle and have conflicts about making sound decisions. It will be difficult for you to step back and not interfere during these times, but be supportive and allow them the space they need to come to their own conclusions.

Most of you already have what it takes to be effective teachers and models for your children. What most often gets in the way is your anxiety and fear of failure. When you are anxious, you tend to be more rigid and inflexible. You may be unable to take your role in stride, or you may lack the confidence to follow through on the commitments you make about child-rearing. In any case, your confusion and anxiety will be passed on to your sons and daughters. Your youngsters will in turn become anxious and fearful. They may show their anxiety by being extremely shy or "acting out" aggressive behavior. Each action is an attempt to avoid or deny their uncomfortable feelings. They are insecure and confused by your attitudes and behavior and may be in conflict about their own perception of what is happening. During periods of extreme anxiety, their world will be distorted. Reassure them. Help them to create a calm, steady environment so that they will not feel out of control.

Remember that your children will always pick up on emotional feelings first and react to them long before they ever hear your words.

Common Problem Areas: Potential Battlegrounds

All families deal with some predictable and common issues, and adoptive families are no exception.

Your children may attempt to involve you and your spouse in conflicts over them. They may try to force you to take sides with them and against each other. *Do not allow them to manipulate you.* If you disagree with your spouse, talk about it in private. Decide together how you will handle the problem. Do not fall into the trap of your child's telling you that Mommy or Daddy said they could do something. Check it out first with your spouse. Present a united front.

Do not cooperate when children try to involve you in a power struggle with them or with your spouse. If there is no reinforcement, they will usually stop trying. When children do not succeed with this behavior in early years, they usually drop it. Your youngsters will abandon useless behaviors as they learn new ways of communicating.

Bedtime

Your toddlers and preschoolers will sometimes use bedtime as a way of gaining additional attention from you. They may develop elaborate rituals to keep you attentive and by their side. They will want water, or need to go to the bathroom, or be afraid of the dark, or not be able to sleep. There are many more excuses.

As parents, you must put a stop to this behavior with firm, consistent direction. Make a clear statement about what you expect. Let your children know that bedtime is not the time to discuss anything. If they get out of bed, escort them back without a word. Gradually, they will know that you are serious about your expectations and will accept bedtime without complaining or trying to engage you. They will know that their actions will be ignored, not rewarded.

Mealtime

Your need to nurture your children is usually very strong; sensing this, they may use food as an object of a power struggle. They may decide not to eat in order to punish you or to attract attention. As soon as you show them that you do not have an investment in whether they eat or not, your children will usually start to eat again. It is also important to note that appetites vary from child to child and from meal to meal. If you have any questions, consult your pediatrician or family doctor.

Attention-Getting

Some adopted children may want to discuss their adoption at times when it is not convenient for you. They may use their questions about adoption as a way of getting your attention or testing you. These queries may come at bedtime, or when you are with your friends, or when you are driving a car filled with other children. Tell your children that you will be happy to talk to them at another time. Be specific as to when this talk will occur. Your youngsters will soon learn that their adoption is not something that they can use to manipulate you.

Parents' Mistakes

You will make mistakes. If you are not aware of your errors, your children will probably let you know about them. Look at these mistakes as opportunities to reassess your goals and expectations. Take them seriously, but do not let them pull you down. Know that errors are inevitable.

Admit your mistakes to yourself. In most situations you can also tell your children. They will respect you for being honest and will view you as a fair and reasonable person. You will also be letting your children know that everyone makes mistakes and learns from them.

When your children err, they are usually attempting to test

their environment or to try out some new-found skill. They are learning about their world and do not always know what will work. Even if you tell them ahead of time not to do something, many children have to see for themselves. Many adopted youngsters have a great need to challenge and test everything in an effort to make a statement about who they are. (We'll learn more about this when we discuss identity issues in chapter 12.) But, whether adopted or not, everyone needs to learn through trial and error, and some youngsters are more curious than others.

Mutually Satisfying Solutions

Your general plan should work if your expectations are age appropriate. Toddlers and preschoolers need direct statements about expectations. Consequences should also be relatively simple and brief. Often a distraction or taking your child away from the situation is all that is needed. Usually they will respond to a "breathing time" of five or ten minutes. Seat them on a chair or send them to their rooms for that brief time.

As your children get older, their level of understanding changes, and they can begin to take a more active part in setting goals. Give them more latitude to learn but make them responsible for their own actions. They must ultimately internalize your controls and guidelines and make them their own.

Never permit your children to physically or verbally abuse you, likewise, you should not abuse them. If you are unable to stop yourself from hitting or abusing them, seek professional help immediately. Many therapists and support groups are available to assist you. Also seek professional help if your youngsters persist in hitting or abusing you and you have set limits.

As young children learn what is expected of them, they should have opportunities to test the behaviors and try again. Eventually they will make their own appropriate decisions. If you create the climate for experimenting, they will learn what is right for them.

Learning often involves making choices. You can help them

make good decisions by giving them acceptable choices. For example, if your children prepare their own snacks or bake cookies and always leave a mess in the kitchen, you may give them a choice of cleaning up or not baking. The choice is theirs. They take responsibility for their own actions. Do not make threats: issue a statement. Once the expectation is clearly stated, you must follow through. In time, you can give them another opportunity to test what they have learned—that they are accountable for their own behavior.

Very young children (two- to five-year-olds) continuously test their environment. They don't take "no" for an answer very easily and will often stage a tantrum when they do not get their way, whether they want a cookie before dinner or dislike getting dressed in the morning. When young children have tantrums, they are usually expressing anger. Try saying to them, "If you want to stay here with me, you must stop screaming. Otherwise, go to your room until you're finished. Then if you would like to tell me why you are so angry, we can talk about it." You have given them a choice. They have also learned that you are not criticizing their feelings, only how they are being displayed. If tantrums are controlled in the early years, they usually will not persist.

You may find that you will need to negotiate with older children (age seven and older). They may introduce ideas that you had not initially considered. You may not always agree with them, but if you listen to what they have to say, they will get the message that although their opinions have merit and you respect them as individuals, what you say goes.

There will be times when it will be hard to say "no" to your children. They may want to do something that you believe is not appropriate for them or that they may not be ready to encounter. Your love for them will help you set the limits. They may be angered by your decision, but you will know that you have done what you believe is correct.

Occasionally a child will not respond to natural consequences and, when given choices, will not always make the right decisions or learn from his or her actions and mistakes. Usually these youngsters react well to incentives rather than consequences. You can motivate them to behave in acceptable ways by allowing them to earn special privileges. Work out a program and make them part of the process. Chart their progress so that they can actually see how they are doing.

The Incentive Chart

I have used the following chart successfully. It works best with children five to ten years old.

(Child's Name) CAN MAKE PROGRESS

	M	T	W	Th	F	Sat	Sun
I *can:* Wake up on time							
Make my bed							
Brush my teeth							
Put my dirty clothes in the hamper							
Keep my clean clothes folded neatly							
Pay attention in class							
Respect my friends							
Be gentle with my sister/brother							

Total Weekly Points Earned _____

If you decide to use an incentive chart, start with three or four behaviors that you would like to change. Keep the wording positive (for example, "I can") and simple. Tell your children about your plan and how the charts will work. You may decide to reward them with a special privilege or gift after they have earned a certain number of points. Set out weekly incentives at the beginning, and then gradually increase the time frame. Some rewards may take a month to earn. Choose incentives that have meaning to your children: playing with a close friend, sleeping over at a friend's house, going to a birthday party. (Never use your child's own birthday as a reward or consequence. A birthday is special and should never be taken away.)

Use the incentive chart only when natural and logical consequences do not work. With these charts, your children will learn what is expected of them. When they establish a habit of behaving the way you want them to, you can gradually eliminate the charts.

When to Seek Professional Help

There may be times when, no matter what you do, your children will still not behave in an acceptable manner. You may find that what worked in the past is no longer suitable, and you feel "stuck." Or, you may believe that you have not become the parents you had hoped to be. Occasionally you will deal with crises within the family that have had a profound effect on everyone or on one child in particular.

Here are fifteen instances when you will need to seek professional help:

1. Your infertility nags at you.
2. You strive for perfection.
3. You feel overwhelmed as a parent.
4. You have a strong-willed child who does not respond to your guidance.
5. You are dealing with disharmony within your marriage. Poor marital relationships create anxious children.
6. You experience a major crisis in the family: the loss of a job, a move to a new home or school, a death in the family, major illness.
7. Your children have problems in school.
8. Your youngsters have poor peer relationships.
9. You emotionally or physically abuse your children.

10. Your children emotionally or physically abuse you.
11. Your youngsters are unusually active.
12. Your son or daughter is depressed, has lost interest in life, or has attempted suicide.
13. You become overly concerned about adoption issues.
14. Your children are overly concerned about their adoption, and you are not able to comfort them.
15. Your child's behavior, personality, and friends change dramatically. You may be encountering a drug or alcohol problem. (This will be addressed more fully in chapter 11, "Help! Help! I have a Teenager.")

Your physician, pediatrician, and family therapist can help when you cannot cope. Let these professionals assist you in dealing with the complex and challenging job of parenting.

All parents are concerned about their family's well-being. Many adoptive parents become either unduly anxious about problems that occur with their children or deny that they exist. It seems that these couples are unable to come to terms with the everyday issues that all families face. Their inability to accept the fact that they can be different from other parents when it comes to adoption but the same in all other areas gets in the way of their parenting.

Don't let this happen to you. Stay tuned in to what is really taking place in your family. You will deal with problems that are directly related to adoption as well as those that are just part of being parents. If you become overly anxious, you will create anxiety in your children, and eventually they will either shut you out and not listen or will feel ineffectual. When you deny that problems exist, you risk the possibility that the issues will get out of hand.

A few adoptive parents continuously focus on their children's biological background. For example, if there has been offensive or even criminal behavior in the biofamily, they worry that their child will grow up and be just like their biomother or biofather. Don't let your fears rule you. After all, all children are individuals. (The next chapter will focus on questions of heredity and environment.)

Be aware. Check your family's emotional temperature from

time to time. Look for the formation of patterns of unacceptable behavior. Pay attention to what you see and hear. Catch the problems before they become too serious. Seek the help you need when your guidelines don't work.

You can be successful parents and raise your youngsters to become morally responsible adults.

III

Discovering an Identity

9

Nature or Nurture

The nature-nurture dilemma has been around for a long time. We can look back to Plato and Aristotle and see each camp support its beliefs with sound documentation. The nature enthusiasts claim that heredity is the main source of an individual's personality and behavior. Those who favor nurture are proponents of the environment shaping and forming who we are.

Over the years, psychological theory and thought has moved back and forth between heredity and environment, depending on whose hypotheses are currently in favor. A great deal of evidence has been presented to support each of the theories and beliefs, which have had a profound influence on parents and children.

Both adoptive and biological parents have swung with the pendulum. In the past, mothers and fathers were told that heredity and "genes" were everything. Children were who they were because of who their biological parents were. In fact, children were expected to be just like their parents. There was little room for individual differences, and those who did not conform to the family mold were labeled the "black sheep" or the "bad seed."

Environmentalists took the lead in the early 1950s. Parents were told that they could mold their children into anything they wanted them to become. With the right reinforcement and appropriate shaping of behavior, every child could be what his or her parents expected. Parents took their task seriously, and when their youngsters did not shape up, they blamed themselves.

Today, the environmentalists are losing favor, and the proponents of heredity are making statements about how genes influence who an individual becomes. Again, research studies are being used to confirm their hypotheses. These data often come from researchers' work with adopted children and twins who were raised apart.

How does all of this affect the adoptive family?

Until recently, adoptive couples were given little information about their children's heritage. When they adopted through agencies, an attempt was made to "match" parents and children, but little data were made available to the adoptive parents. They were told that the environmental influences were of great significance and that behavior, for the most part, was shaped by outside factors, not genes.

Yet, many adoptive parents began to observe personalities and temperaments in their infants and young children that were their own. As these children grew older, it became evident that their individuality had little relationship to how they were raised by their adoptive family.

From all of the research data, psychological theory, and parents' observations, we have learned that there are powerful factors that influence personality and behavior. Let's first look at the part heredity plays in this complex puzzle.

Heredity—the Unknown Factor

Until recently, adoptive couples had little information about their children's heritage. Even today, information given to them at the time of placement may be limited or censored. Most of what is available is usually told to the social worker by the bioparents or is exchanged at the time the adoptive parents interview them. In either case, the communication is usually of a general nature.

And so, as adoptive parents, you will begin your relationship with your children with many unknowns.

As you study the little strangers in your arms, you will begin to look for something familiar with which to connect. As the close emotional bond forms, you will search for some common features. In all relationships, people will try to find in others characteristics that they can share. When meeting someone for the first time, we all wonder "What is this person like? How is he like me? Will we hit it off?" For parents and their children, the need to relate is crucial to their understanding and communication.

You may be frustrated by the differences you see between you and your children. You will be surprised by unexpected behavior, and many times will watch in awe as your youngster's personality emerges. At each age and stage of your child's development, you find unanticipated actions and personality traits.

No parent can foresee what his children will be like, but the adoptive parent must deal with more unpredictable variables. In most biological families, children can be understood in terms of their resemblance to their parents or other family members. Parents can say, "He's like his Uncle Henry" or "She's just like Cousin Jenny." These similarities allow them to better understand their child.

As adoptive parents, you can best get to know your youngsters by being open to the possibility that:

HEREDITY PLAYS AN IMPORTANT ROLE
IN PERSONALITY DEVELOPMENT.

Medical Data

Adoptive families often have little information about the medical history of their child's biofamily. Both parents and adoptees have expressed the need to have more medical data. Their desire to know usually comes out of a real fear of the unknown and repeated situations in which this medical information is required.

When medical forms must be completed, the adoptive family often must write "unknown" in answer to many of the questions. Adult adoptees continue to leave blank many spaces in their medical histories. Adoptive parents and their children are afraid that these unknowns could become health hazards and risks about which they would have no knowledge. Continuing evidence shows that many high-risk diseases that run in families can be treated with preventative medicine, *if known.*

Limited information about health is common in adoptive families despite increasing evidence that shows a genetic contribution to many diseases. Conditions such as allergies, diabetes, heart disease, hypertension, learning disorders, and hearing deficiencies can be treated effectively early in a child's life. Even bed-wetting has a genetic component and can be traced through families. Many anxious parents have agonized over the possibility of being responsible for severe psychological harm when their children wet their beds. If genetic information is available, much pain and suffering could be alleviated.

Significant data indicate that a person can be predisposed not only to physical illness but also to emotional illness. Recent studies have shown that alcohol and substance abuse also have a genetic base.

If you had more knowledge of your child's heritage, you would be better able to anticipate any factors that could be potential problems and be ready to deal with them before they occurr. Many of the answers are available, and the adoptive couple usually has the opportunity to find out about them. It is also possible to ask the biofamilies to update the case file with any significant information as it occurs over the years. You can do this through your attorney or social worker.

Tastes and Talents

A knowledge of what talents and abilities run in your child's biological family may also be relevant and have significant consequences. Your child would often carry the same capabilities. If you have all of the facts, you will be in a better position to make informed decisions about your son or daughter.

When adult adoptees and their biofamilies have reunions, it is always interesting to observe how much adoptees have in common with their biomothers and biofathers. They may physically resemble one another and they may also have the same tastes and preferences. (We will discuss this further in chapter 13.)

Temperament

As stated earlier, children's temperaments can be observed at birth. We can see those differences in the hospital nursery as we watch the infant who naps quietly, the one who sleeps fitfully, or the one who is wide awake. These babies have begun to make statements to the world about how they will respond to it. They will be aggressive or shy, noisy or quiet, irritable or satisfied.

All parents must deal with the temperamental differences between them and their children. In biological families those disparities are usually minimal. Occasionally, biological parents must contend with great differences between their children's temperaments and their own. That is the exception, however, and not the rule.

In adoptive families, the dispositions of parents and their children are almost always dissimilar. When you are ready to come to terms with the differences and accept the fact that heredity plays an important part in your children's growth and development, you can begin to consider how environment also plays a role.

Environment Matters

We know from our own experiences that learning can change and affect us. As we watch all children, we see how much of what they learn is motivated or discouraged by different environmental factors. When they have successful experiences, their efforts are reinforced, and they are pushed to attempt new things. If they fail, they may hesitate to try again. Harsh punishment will make them fearful so that they move on to new activities with less enthusiasm.

For many years, there was a universal acceptance by many educators, therapists, and parents that the environment was the major determinant of behavior. A great deal of blame was placed on parents and society for deviances and problem children. In many instances, since the mother was the primary caregiver, much of the responsibility for her child's actions was on her shoulders. She was looked at as the most powerful force in a child's life. When the child had problems, they became the mother's fault. Of course, if the child was a model of behavior, the mother could also take full credit.

Today, proponents of the environment as the major factor in shaping behavior believe that many outside factors, not only the mother's influence, affect children's actions. As fathers become more involved in child-rearing, they become powerful forces in their children's growth and development. Brothers and sisters also play a significant role in molding behavior.

In addition, influences outside the home are of major consequence in a child's life. Teachers carry great weight as authorities for all children. And as youngsters grow up, their peers can sway them and can influence their decision-making and actions.

Both adoptive and biological parents deal with the environmental pressures on their children, and they come to understand that the parents' part is limited when you consider all of the factors involved.

We do know:

THE ENVIRONMENT PLAYS AN IMPORTANT ROLE IN
PERSONALITY DEVELOPMENT.

The Interplay of Nature and Nurture

Both heredity and environment are important in forming the individual. To what degree one factor is more significant than the other is difficult to determine. As adoptive parents, you may have a dilemma in deciding just how much genetic influences have a part in shaping your children and their behavior.

Most of us know someone who, despite a deprived and nonnurturing environment, has gone on to become a successful and satisfied person. When we look at IQ scores, we can see both genes and environment at work. Many educators can attest to the influence of the environment on both intelligence and school performance; however, predisposition is a key to many abilities.

It really does not matter whether heredity or environment plays a more important role in your children's growth and development as long as you remember that both factors are of major significance. Adoptive parents usually have a problem in deciding which of their children's behaviors are primarily genetic and how much influence they really have in shaping their youngsters.

If you have a lot of details about your child's genetic heritage, you can make informed decisions as he or she grows and changes. You do not have to be plagued with doubts about your parenting skills and can move ahead with confidence. Remember: Heredity *creates* characteristics and environment *modifies* them.

How to Make Heredity and Environment Work Together

You have a unique opportunity as adoptive parents to be objective about your children and who they really are. Most biological families have preconceived ideas about their youngsters and the adults they will become. They take a great deal for granted and may not always be open to differences between their children and themselves. Their biases create conflicts within their families when their children do not conform to expectations.

Parents who are not subjective about their children are in a good position to help them grow to become happy, satisfied adults. Adoptive parents have the best advantage because they can maintain an objectivity that many other parents do not have.

In order to make heredity and environment work for you and your family:

- Accept the fact that heredity plays an important part in who your children are.
- Know that environment has a powerful influence over your youngsters.

You can understand your children's biological heritage if you:

- Gain as much information at the time of placement as possible. (Additional data may be available through your state's bureau of adoptions. You will get no identifying information but may be able to fill in some gaps.)

• Observe your youngsters as they grow and change.
• Allow your children to become the individuals they were meant to be.
• Let your children make mistakes as they test and try new possibilities. You will all learn from this process.

Your role as adoptive parent is to:

• Guide your children on their particular paths of discovery.
• Expose them to many possibilities so that they may choose the right ones for themselves.
• Know that you are only one of the many environmental factors involved.
• Encourage, support, and appreciate your youngsters.
• Expect them to be different from you.
• Accept them for who they are.

It is important to always consider that both heredity and environment are working together to create the individual. Assume that nature and nurture collaborate as your youngsters grow and develop into adults. There will be times when you will be actively involved in the process; at other times you will step back as your children teach you who they are becoming.

As you watch and learn, you will see your children experience the dynamic process of growing up.

10

Puberty Is
a Stormy Condition

Ellen, age eleven, came home from school, ran into her room, and slammed the door shut. Her parents, Jean and Mike, were alarmed by Ellen's behavior, and when they tried to talk to her, she refused to come out of her room.

Finally, after much coaxing, Ellen told her parents that she had homework to do that she was unable to complete and would probably get an "F" grade. Jean and Mike assured her that they would assist her with whatever was needed. Ellen was convinced that no one could help her. She threw her books on the floor, sat on her bed, and began to sob.

After some time, she shared her problem with Jean and Mike. Her teacher had asked the class to bring their birth certificates to school the next day. When Jean assured her that she would give Ellen a copy of the certificate, Ellen told her that it was not her *real* birth certificate because it did not have the names of her *real* parents on it.

At first, Jean and Mike were hurt by what their daughter was saying, but as the dialogue continued, it was obvious to them that Ellen was angry because she did not know who her bioparents were. When they supported Ellen's feelings, she became calmer. She left for school the next day with the required document, but it was not until several years later that Ellen was really able to talk freely about the feelings that had engulfed her that day.

Mike, Jean, and Ellen were dealing with a typical problem that all adoptive parents face during the turbulent years of puberty. Although the scenario may be different for each family, the angry feelings that Ellen expressed are a part of all adopted children. Their anger stems from a sense of helplessness over not knowing their biological roots. They are confused and uncertain about much of their life at this time, and their adoption adds to the muddle. Their awareness, perception, and understanding of the world is emerging from a child's limited vision to that of the adult they are yet to become.

Your children may display their feelings in diverse ways, and if you are open to listening, as Jean and Mike were, you will hear what they have to say. You will also experience what all families encounter as their children move into their teen years. For most children, one stormy event will usher in the beginning of puberty. Adopted children may use their adoption to express the changes that they are going through, but they could just as easily have used any one of a number of other issues. What all pubescent youngsters, whether adopted or biological, have in common is their unpredictability.

For most of you, your previous experiences with your children may have been relatively calm and noneventful. Your children's early years most likely evolved with the predictable "growing pains." Probably your children had a moderate amount of problems in their younger years, but for the most part they were basically "good kids." Then, without warning, you will become part of the turbulence that accompanies the onset of puberty. Some of you may have already encountered major upsets with your children, and puberty will exacerbate any preexisting condition.

For all families, the onset of puberty jolts even the most stable of family relationships. Each situation that presents itself will seem to be completely out of character for your child. Totally unexpected and unprecedented events will occur. You will find yourself caught off guard, as if the rug had been pulled out from under you. From that moment on, the relationship between you and your child will change and will remain uncertain for several years. The equilibrium of the past will be disrupted, and the rapport that you originally had with your child will be broken.

You will never be able to go back to the former patterns that worked; instead, you will have to find new ways of relating to your children. Toward the end of the teen years, a fresh foundation will gradually develop that will be the basis for the relationship that you and your children will follow into their adulthood. But for now, you will be moving through a period of fluctuation and change, and during the throes of puberty, you will not find it easy to look ahead.

It will be difficult for you to be objective about your experiences during these years. Even the most well-informed parents will not be able to understand why their once open and friendly children are now sullen and isolated in their rooms. Children who just yesterday were affectionate and loving may rebuff you when you try to put your arms around them or when you reach out in the most loving of gestures.

You will certainly feel helpless and frustrated during the next several years. There will be times when you will anguish over your children's behavior as you try to understand what is happening.

Like all parents of children who are going through puberty, you will experience:

- Your children's unpredictable behavior.
- Your children's outbursts of strong emotion.
- Few periods of quiescence.
- Your children's temper tantrums.
- Your own disbelief.
- Doubts about your parenting abilities.
- Your frequent loss of composure.
- Recurrent moments of helplessness.
- Exasperation, anger, rage, and emotions you never thought you would experience.
- Guilt about feeling the way you do.

As adoptive parents, you will experience:

- All of the above.
- Your children's confusion, helplessness, and anger about their adoption.
- Your own thoughts and feelings about their adoption.
- Doubts about your effectiveness as an adoptive parent.

Here is some of what you can expect during this stage of development.

Physical Changes

You will be swept into puberty along with your children. The changes that take place in an individual between the beginning of puberty and adulthood are immense, and your child will be no exception. The adolescent years act as a major landmark for most people—a rite of passage—and this time carries with it the painful tasks of initiation into maturity. All pubescent children undergo rapid and erratic physical and hormonal transformations, and they will react to those unexpected and fluctuating changes with erratic responses. It will be as if they must first resist and then accept each change within themselves.

Spurts of Growth

Once you have acknowledged that your child has begun puberty, your family can be better prepared by knowing just what physical changes are actually taking place. They will occur in spurts and can be recognized through appearance and behavior. You will actually see your youngsters grow in stature, weight, and strength. In addition, your children's major organs will gradually enlarge. Their digestive and reproductive systems will also reach their potential, and secondary sexual characteristics will appear. Hormonal changes that occur simultaneously further exaggerate and add to your adolescent's development.

What will be most startling to some of you is that your child can begin the stage of puberty as early as eight years old; others may not show any signs of change until they are sixteen.

Check with your physician if you are in doubt or have any questions.

Girls may have more difficulty in adjusting to the physiological changes of puberty if they mature at either an early age or very late. Boys also experience problems if they mature late.

At whatever age puberty occurs, you and your youngsters will encounter the most severe stresses during the periods when the greatest physical changes take place. It helps to let your children know what is physically changing within them. Many children are frightened when they don't understand what is happening to them. Although your dialogue may allay some of their fears, it will not eliminate the turmoil that seems to be inevitable during puberty.

Where Is the Child I Once Knew?

Where is my little girl
The one I knew before
Whose happy face and smiling eyes
I'll love forever more.

Who is this person now
Her face and eyes familiar
Whose happiness is rarely seen
A stranger from afar.

What makes my life so empty
Without that child so real
A void, a pain, a longing
For her laughter's special peal.

Why has she turned from me
A stranger, so alone
Tears and anger replacing
The tenderness we'd known.

How can I share today
My love and need of her

When gestures of deep feelings
Cause not the slightest stir.

My hope is for tomorrow
When she will smile with me
No longer child, but woman
In full maturity.

I wrote this poem for my daughter during the throes of her early teen years. As we both grappled with the unknowns and the uncertainties of those turbulent times, I wondered if I ever would be able to relate to her as one adult to another. Today, I can see that it is possible but at that time I had many doubts.

Mood Swings

What can you expect from your children during puberty?

For the most part, your youngsters, like all children, will experience major mood swings, which will affect their behavior and actions. They will move from periods of aggression and turmoil to relatively calm, quiescent relief. During these quiet spells, you will believe that they have moved out of this juncture in time. Just when you experience a sense of relief that it is all over and think you can be a normal family again, your youngsters will remind you that they are not finished with this stage of development. Once again you will have to deal with another problem, mood, or unexpected event. Each time this behavior occurs, you will not be prepared and will be initially overwhelmed.

While you try to come to terms with what is happening, your young adolescent will attempt to make sense of what he or she is experiencing. Unable to understand their great mood swings, they may develop intense feelings of anxiety about the sudden changes they observe in themselves. Even though you have alerted them to what is taking place, they will still be unable to tolerate their emotions. They seem to act first without thinking, only to discover that their behavior does not make the anxious feelings go away. It's as if they have been propelled into action like a switch being turned on, and they don't have the ability to turn off, only to wind down in time.

Me, Myself, and I

Pubescent youngsters are thoroughly engrossed in their bodies, image, and appearance. They will spend hours looking into a mirror, checking for the slightest blemish: a pimple, a hair out of place, an uneven hemline. As they appraise themselves, they become increasingly self-critical. Their obsession with their looks takes over at times, and nothing can dissuade them from believing that they are ugly. They will refuse to face the world in this condition, only to go out with a friend a moment later, after trying on an entire wardrobe, which has been left in a heap on their bedroom floor.

Adolescents are convinced that the world should center around them and when it does not, they become enraged and might even tell you that you don't love them or don't care about them. They may demand your attention to prove to themselves that they are lovable. After all, how can anyone love someone who is so ugly? An instant later, they will thrust you aside as they did their unwanted clothing. Throughout all of these ups and downs, you will be tugged and pulled at, trying to maintain a balance and make sense of what is going on. It is important to remember that all families, whether adoptive or not, will have similar experiences.

Relationships

When your children are not forcing their needs upon you, they will ignore you or withdraw from you. As they move into puberty, their peers will have enormous power over them. Their friends and the group they belong to will have more influence than you will ever have again. With their friends, they will reevaluate and test past values against their present reality. There will be times when they will reject those values that you hold dear so that they can be accepted by their peers.

Young adolescents try to understand and find their own way in the world. One day they may tell you that they are running away from home because you don't understand them; the following week, they will threaten to go to their room and never come out. You will struggle as they do, trying to define and redefine the relationship you now have with them.

Your son or daughter will be completely crushed when a

friend slights him or her and then become furious at you when you try to comfort. You will get caught up in their emotional outbursts only to find that they have resolved their conflicts without your help.

The children you once knew may be so different now that you will wonder how they could have changed so drastically. In your bewilderment you will attempt to grasp at reasons for the radical shift in temperament and behavior. If you attempt to discuss the dramatic transformation with them, they will probably become defensive or question your perception. They might tell you that these times are different from those of your adolescence and that they are fine and you just do not know what is really going on—you just "don't understand."

Adolescents appear to be very sure of themselves on the surface, and they will imply that you are the one who is changing or not understanding or all wrong. They will disarm you with their comments, and you will be the one who is left feeling unsure and wondering "Where did I go wrong?" While you struggle with your feelings, they will be very self-righteous and convinced that they are "right."

As you pick yourself up and gather yourself together again, your young adolescent will be off on another tangent with the same intensity and erratic behavior. It will seem as if you have no respite from the barrage of emotion and kinetic energy around you. You will feel weary and powerless to combat the profound forces of puberty.

The Teeter-Totter of Puberty

As you and your children struggle through puberty together, keep in mind that *your children:*

- Experience substantial physical changes.
- Undergo spurts of growth, not steady, moderate changes.
- Grow outside (body size) and inside (major organs).
- Try to accommodate the transformations.
- Are overwhelmed and anxious about what is happening to them.
- Become adults.

Understand that as parents *you:*

• Try to adjust and accommodate.
• Are overwhelmed and anxious.
• Are impatient with their slow and sporadic development.
• Are just like all other parents during this development stage.

The Real Meaning of Adoption

Puberty and adolescence are the most complicated and trying periods for all families, and the adoptive family has many more issues to compound the problems. Both you and your children are forced to confront the subject of adoption more realistically than you have ever done before. You will assess and reappraise yourself and your youngsters, look for answers, hope for solutions and a peaceful resolution, and wonder if your family will ever be normal again.

Sometime during puberty, your children will become fully aware of the real meaning of adoption. Before this time, they understood adoption in the limited way all children comprehend complex ideas. They already knew that they were different from many other children because they were adopted, but they had no conception of what that really meant. You had told them that adoption was special, and they had believed you. Now they will question that specialness and struggle with new information. As they get in touch with their own sexuality and try to make sense of it, they will grapple with their own adoption and what it means.

> When Jeremy ran away from home, he was only twelve years old. Patti and Don were beside themselves. They were shocked and confused by their son's behavior. Prior to this incident, Jeremy had begun to withdraw from the family, isolating himself in his room for many hours.
>
> Patti and Don believed that Jeremy's seclusion was an indication that he was beginning his teenage "stage," and they felt prepared to handle anything that

came their way. They had always been open in their communication with Jeremy about all issues, including his adoption.

They were not ready for a runaway.

They tormented themselves for three days, calling his friends, contacting the police. Then Jeremy returned home. Fortunately no harm had befallen him, but he was very different from the person he had been before he left. The quiet, sullen boy had become angry and belligerent. Nothing seemed to comfort him, not a kind word or a loving hug.

Patti and Don felt stuck.

When the family first came to me for therapy, Jeremy seemed unreachable. He sat with his arms folded and his body slightly turned away from the rest of us; he was determined not to say a word. It was clear that he was angry, but he was also hurting a great deal, although no one was really sure what was causing his pain.

After several months in therapy, Jeremy began to open up. The reluctant boy became more verbal as he began to relax. What he said made it clear that his running away was an attempt to escape from his feelings about being adopted.

His emotions were varied and complex. It was difficult for him to understand how anyone could "give up" a baby. He felt rejected, and he was angry about that. He decided that the only way a mother could abandon her child was if there were something wrong with that child. He questioned his value and self-worth.

At the same time, he judged his parents' decision to adopt him. Did they know that he was defective? How could they love him? Maybe they, too, had deficiencies that would allow them to totally accept him.

How could he love them? They were so different from him. They didn't understand him. Did they really know him? Who was he, anyway? Only his biomother knew. His biomother would understand him. She could help him find out who he really was. She would take away the pain and make him feel better.

And then the questions would begin again. . . . How could his biomother have left him? The guilt, the anguish, and the hurt would return. He repeated the original abandonment by running away from the only parents he had ever known. He could get even that way.

Over a period of several years, Jeremy was able to come to terms with the initial trauma and begin to know himself and like the person he was becoming. He expressed regret at not having more information about his heritage, but felt that he would not want to search for and meet his bioparents when he became an adult. (Search and reunion are discussed in chapter 13.)

Jeremy struggled with powerful feelings of rejection and abandonment during his early teen years. Patti and Don were available to give him support along the way, but they felt inadequate and helpless through much of that time. When Jeremy rejected himself, he also cast off his parents. It was difficult for him to accept their love when he felt so defective.

As Jeremy learned about himself, he was able to accept his parents; however, they all became acutely aware of the significant dissimilarities between them. Jeremy had an identity that was his own. Even though they had all wanted to believe that Jeremy was his own person, the family had also hoped that they could have a great deal in common.

The strong emotions that impacted Jeremy and his family are typical of what most adoptive families experience. Although the feelings may manifest themselves in diverse ways, your family will probably face the same issues. All children experience confusion and uncertainty about their identities during the teen years, and their families must deal with tensions during this time of development. Adoptive families, however, go through this period with more intense and pronounced difficulties.

Real Moms and Dads

As your youngsters begin to learn more about themselves, they will continue to test and question everything and everyone around them. They will tell you that their friends' parents are more lenient, more indulgent, even more understanding. They will attempt to convince you that other parents allow their children to do things that you will not permit. They might say, "If you were my *real* mom, you'd understand" or "I don't have to listen to you, you're not my *real* dad."

Adopted children usually talk about "real" moms and dads when they sense that their parents feel particularly vulnerable as adoptive parents. Young teenagers will always try to test your authority and question whether you love them. They seem to be saying, "If you really love me, I can do anything and it won't destroy your feelings for me."

As their behavior becomes progressively worse, they wait to be rejected by you as they once were by their bioparents. When you do not respond favorably to their actions, they perceive your negative responses as proof of your rejection, and the spiraling process continues.

Your function as "real" parents may be challenged at other times as well.

> Cindy liked to daydream. Throughout her young childhood, as all children do, she had imagined herself in many situations, some plausible and others, completely unrealistic.
>
> Many times, Cindy wondered what it would have been like if she had been adopted into another family. She envisioned the preferential treatment she would get—the special gifts bestowed on her and the life of bliss she would lead.
>
> When Cindy was thirteen years old, she began to verbalize her fantasies, first to her friends, and then to her parents. Mary and Rick believed that they had failed Cindy in some way. They wondered how their child could want a different family, and they were deeply hurt when she said, "What if someone else had adopted me?"
>
> Mary and Rick talked about their problem in their adoptive parent support group and found that other families were hearing similar statements from their youngsters. Many of them were perplexed about how to deal with the issue.
>
> Finally, one mother told the group how she handled the dilemma. When her daughter made a statement to

her about what it might have been like if someone else had adopted her, she answered, "I guess those are the breaks."

Mary and Rick were trying to cope with the typical musings of their teenage daughter. Certainly, your child's thoughts should be taken seriously, but when there is really no obvious possibility of changing a situation, accept it and move on. Your youngsters will take the cue from you. They can dream as much as they want. You can help them deal with reality.

Part of coming to terms with what is real is to understand what underlies your teenager's behavior. Their adoption is bewildering to them during their teen years. It is difficult for them to understand much about "sex" anyway, and it is incomprehensible to them that anyone could reject a baby. So, when they consider that a man and a woman conceived them and then gave them up, they take it as a rejection. No matter what you do or say, they will feel deeply hurt about having been relinquished.

The words *relinquishment* and *put up* for adoption have been replaced in recent years by the word *placement;* however, no matter what words are used to describe adoption, your teenager will still feel abandoned, relinquished, and rejected. These early teen years will be the most difficult for all of you. Your youngsters will take this time in their lives to work through their feelings about being adopted. You can help them by understanding that what they are experiencing is a necessary part of growing up, and you cannot "make it better" for them. They must struggle through this period until they reach a position of acceptance.

Your children must know that they have a safe place in which to deal with their powerful feelings about adoption. If the right atmosphere is not available to them, they will only postpone what they must ultimately face. As parents, you can always provide opportunities for your children to explore their profound emotions. They may not always take you up on your availability to listen, but they need to know that you are there and that you understand.

Your Role as Parents

The early teen years will be very trying ones for you. Your role as parents will be continuously questioned and tested. The short period of puberty will seem interminable as you attempt to deal with the issues. You will wonder if you have the right answers and be able to cope with the problems. Your youngsters' anxieties about the changes within themselves will trigger new doubts and concerns for you. You may even feel like a failure as a parent. Don't.

As your children act out new and unexpected behaviors, your feelings of self-doubt will add further tension to an already stressful situation. With each new problem, you may find that you do not have all of the answers, and when the issues are resolved, you may wonder what part you actually did play.

Realize that you and your spouse may not see "eye to eye" on dealing with these problems, and each unexpected event could become a test of your marriage. Your adolescent may try to play each of you against the other, appealing to the one who is most lenient or is most anxious.

How can you maintain a balance in your lives when erratic outbursts and unexpected problems continually confront you? Remember that each of you is acting out of a sense of helplessness. You will be critical of each other, and your youngster will incessantly question and judge you as well.

Here's a four-step plan to follow when you find that you are having conflicts with your spouse over your children.

1. Define the problem.
2. Discuss the issue with your spouse only.
3. Determine what is interfering with your decision making.
4. Decide together on an equitable solution.

As you confer:

- Do not allow your children to be present.
- Understand and accept each other's style of dealing with problems.

- Be prepared to negotiate with your spouse.
- Keep in mind your son's or daughter's best interest.
- Realize that your differences do not have to interfere with your decision.
- Consider your son's or daughter's feelings.
- Know that your children may get angry at you when you tell them what you expect.
- Believe that a disagreement between you and your children will not make or break the relationship.

You will find as your son or daughter moves through puberty that the differences between you will become more apparent. What you considered minor dissimilarities in the past will become blatantly disparate. Just as Patti and Don came to terms with Jeremy's individuality, you must face your children's strong statements about their identity during puberty. All children will try not to be like their parents and find their own uniqueness. The reality is that adopted youngsters *are* most assuredly different from their parents. If you have not already come to terms with the fact that your children are not like you, puberty is the time when you are forced to accept this reality. Both biological and adoptive parents must face the disparities between themselves and their children, and puberty is the time when those dissimilarities become strikingly apparent.

Along with the pronounced differences that you will see will be an awareness that some of the expectations you had for your children will not be realized. You may have to adjust your plans and goals, accepting the real individuals that your children are becoming. Take another look at them and see them as they really are. Look them over again. They may please you, or you may experience some disappointment. Now is the time to reconcile your feelings so that you can help them through the remaining years of childhood into adulthood. Your children need your guidance and support to find out who they really are.

11

Help! Help!
I Have a Teenager

"Why did you shave one side of your head?"
"Wear your seatbelt!"
"Your girlfriend may not sleep in your room."
"Will we ever see eye to eye?"
"I am NOT square."
"The older my child gets, the dumber I feel."

Most of you will make all, some, or a variation of the above remarks at least once during your children's teenage years. Puberty was just the beginning. Now you have a full-blown adolescent.

Adolescence follows puberty with no warning signs or blaring alarms. It will walk in on the tail end of pubescence with a steady, forceful persistence and will continue relentlessly until your child reaches adulthood. These years are the most challenging for you as a parent. You will find that you have limited influence over your teenagers as they make powerful statements about their individual styles, value systems, and reasoning. Adolescents are provocative, forceful, and unyielding as they follow the path to adulthood.

As adoptive parents, you will play a key role in the process. Before we consider your position, however, let's take a closer look at all adolescents.

116

Adolescents as Social Beings

Adolescents are preparing to leave the nest. They are both excited and anxious about the prospect of living their own lives and being out in the world. The decisions they make now may have far-reaching effects on their lives. At a time when they know little about themselves, they must make some life decisions about careers, training skills, and college.

Most adolescents look to their peers to help them set goals and lay out objectives. They will struggle to make choices for themselves rather than go to their parents for input. Their friends will continue to be the most important single influence on them.

The primary struggle for all adolescents is that of dependence versus independence. All teenagers want to be autonomous, but must continuously confront their feelings about being dependent on their parents. The push-pull of this period becomes a constant theme for your family.

Peers play an important part in the lives of most teenagers. They will want to act, talk, and dress like one another and be together all of the time. There is little room for parents and family. Friends have more influence over a teenager than anyone else ever had. Peer power is stronger than that of any parent, family, or school. How friends think and feel affects how a teenager perceives the world.

The adolescent is passionate about causes, especially those relating to personal rights. They are outraged by human suffering and seek equality and fair play in society and in the world. Their protests are usually loud and urgent, and they keep them up until justice is done. They will join marches, marathons, rallies, and protests in an effort to make a declaration.

As adoptive parents, you will find that your teenagers will make the same strong pronouncements. Your son or daughter is moving into adulthood along the same predictable path. Your teenager will develop into his or her own person, changing relationships with you and seeking a new equilibrium in the family structure. Your adolescent will never be a child again.

By the time teenagers complete their adolescence, they will have separated from their parents and become independent, autonomous individuals: They will have a sexual identity and a value system of their own; they will be able to make commitments to a career; and they will be able to form permanent relationships.

Choices

In the struggle through adolescence, teenagers may not always make good decisions for themselves. The friends they choose may not always be in their best interests. Your teenager may want to be with certain friends because they offer something exciting and different and, maybe, dangerous. All teenagers believe that they are all-powerful—that their very beings protect them from being hurt. In this omnipotent state, they believe that they will not become addicted if they try drugs; they will not get pregnant if they have sex; they will not be hurt if they don't wear seatbelts when they drive.

Your adolescents will tell you that you are "square," "old-fashioned," "out of it." In their state of continuous exploration, they will attempt new experiences, check to see how they fit, and then discard or keep them, depending on their individual personalities, temperaments, and styles of behaving and relating in the world.

Individuality

Your teenager, as all other teenagers, will make strong statements about who he is and what he wants. At the same time that she is trying to be like her friends, she is also attempting to find herself. Teenagers experiment in an attempt to find a unique identity. Their statements appear to be powerful and sure, but they are not yet convinced themselves. By making loud declarations, they actually try to tell themselves that their beliefs, feelings, and thoughts are right for them.

Thinking and Reasoning

All teenagers begin to gain new levels of understanding and logic during adolescence. They are not only growing and changing physically and emotionally but also reaching their maximum levels of cognitive development. The old thought processes of childhood will be abandoned as they move into young adulthood and develop new insights.

You will listen in awe as your adolescent speculates about and considers new ideas. When making decisions, teenagers will look at alternate possibilities, using organized and orderly thoughts. They will make convincing arguments about their convictions and challenge your basic ideals and values as they come to terms with their own attitudes. By the time your children reach adulthood, they will have a unique philosophy of life that has evolved from your influences and those of other life experiences.

The Adopted Teenager

During the experimental phase of adolescence, your adopted child will go through a more profound identity dilemma than will other teenagers (we'll discuss this more in chapter 13). As adoptive parents, you will find that your adolescents explore and test with a greater intensity, almost compulsive. During this predictable but stormy process, your teenagers will strive to make sense of their adoption and who they are. Their strong feelings and opinions may shock and deeply hurt you. They will try to test your love of them by acting out in outrageous and sometimes dangerous ways. At other times, they will demand your love, as if asking, "Will you still love me no matter what I do?" Although a rebellious attitude begins in puberty, it usually intensifies during the remainder of adolescence.

Some of your teenagers will parade in front of you with a strong bravado that belies their real feelings of inadequacy. When you attempt to reach out to them and give them support, they will shrug you off and deny all of their insecurities. Their words and behavior will not always match, and you will end up feeling helpless and inadequate as well.

You will view your children as truly separate from you. The disparities between you will be markedly apparent—what started in puberty is finished in late adolescence. You may need to reach out and reintroduce yourself to become acquainted with this new person in your home. Adolescence will be a startling and awesome experience for you and your youngster. You will look at your teenager with pride, anguish, love, and sometimes hate, experiencing profound feelings of helplessness and knowing that your influence is more limited now than ever before. In just a short time, your child will be a mature individual, and you will glimpse that adult during adolescence.

As you move beyond childhood and through adolescence with your children, how can you be an effective parent?

Parents of Teenagers

As adoptive parents, you have now experienced all of the stages of child development and know that you have a great deal in common with other families. In addition to the periods of joy, stress, pride, and embarrassment that all parents face, you have weathered the stormy times when you had to deal with adoption and you felt not at all like other parents.

Now you will encounter the final stage in your youngster's development. Your influences during this time, as limited as they may be, will still have a profound effect on your son or daughter. As independent as your child may appear, he or she still needs you in many ways.

As you are tested and tried to the limit, you may think about giving up. At other times you will attempt to nurture and comfort your child, hoping that he will respond as he did when he was younger.

The relationship you once had with your child has changed and will never be the same again, but the teen years are when you set the stage for the future. Adolescence will be a period of difficulty and sometimes estrangement, but your role now is a powerful one. Even though you may want to relinquish your position as parent, don't give up now. Hang in there a little longer. Your child still needs you.

You and your spouse also need each other, perhaps now more than ever before. Your marriage may be tested to the limits during your youngster's teenage years. You may be going through crises of your own at this time: dealing with mid-life anxieties, or caring for aging parents. Your spouse may not want to be involved. The best way to survive this upheaval is to work together, negotiate, reach a compromise, stay connected. If you are a single parent, join a support group or attend a seminar or class about raising a teenager. Stay prepared.

Parents as Teachers

Keep the following suggestions in mind when you have conflicts with your adolescents:

- BE STEADY AND SUPPORTIVE.

Give your suggestions and views and allow your teenagers to express theirs. You may not agree with them, but give them as much latitude as you can.

- UNDERSTAND THEIR POSITION.

Whenever possible, come to a compromise. If there is no room for compromise, then stand firm and united with your spouse.

- SET REALISTIC GUIDELINES, NOT BLANKET RULES.
- TAKE EACH SITUATION SEPARATELY.

Sit down and talk about it before you decide on consequences or solutions.

- HAVE A RATIONAL DISCUSSION, WITHOUT STRONG EMOTION.

Your children need your calm steadiness to help them look at the mistakes they have made.

- ALLOW FOR ERRORS.

Your teenagers are still learning and will not always make sound decisions or act appropriately.

- SHOW CONTINUOUS CARING EVEN WHEN THE SITUATION IS LESS THAN TOLERABLE.
- STOP ANY PHYSICAL OR VERBAL ABUSE.

You and your teenager may be very emotional. Cool down before you talk, so you will be able to deal with each other rationally.

Your role as a parent during this stage of development will be the most difficult of all. You will wonder how you can main-

tain a balance in your life when erratic outbursts and unexpected problems confront you. Your feelings and thoughts will
confuse you. As during puberty, there seem to be no *right* answers: What seems right today may be wrong tomorrow. You
managed to get through puberty, however, and you can make
it work just a little bit longer.

You will be critical of your spouse, and your teenager will also
relentlessly criticize and question you. You will be forced to
look at yourself again and again as a parent and as an individual
with strengths and weaknesses. As you become ready to explore
and understand yourself, you should be better equipped to
listen to your adolescent with an open mind, to hear new ideas
and find original solutions.

The goal during the teen years should be to achieve mutual
respect and tolerance with an attitude of open communication
and negotiation. Abandon the rules of the past in favor of a plan
that assesses each situation separately. Solve problems through
flexibility and mutual understanding.

Your Adopted Child

As parents of an adopted child, you can anticipate problems
and crises with your teenager, who will test you to the limit as
do all adolescents. It is very possible that your son or daughter
will be even more trying. Adopted children have a greater struggle throughout their teen years. Starting in puberty, they continuously confront many identity issues and their adoption until
they are able to come to a resolution.

As adopted teenagers come to terms with the issues sur-
rounding adoption, they are forced to grapple with profound
questions concerning who they are (we'll discuss this more in
chapter 13). As they try to find themselves, they may make more
powerful statements than other teenagers. Their actions and
behavior may be more extreme than that of most adolescents.
It will appear as if they are deliberately trying to test you; in
reality, they are experimenting, attempting to make sense of
their identity.

During the teen years, your children will make strong statements about their individuality. They will exaggerate their behavior as they continue to find themselves. You will watch them

go to extremes, propelled into compulsive action in a single-minded mission to find their true selves.

Your youngsters will do bizarre and dangerous things, some of which you will not know about until after the fact. Each event will shock you, leaving you angry and confused. You will wonder how your teenager could expose himself and sometimes you to such terrible risks and hazards. All teenagers will tempt fate and take risks, but your adopted adolescents will often live more dangerously than most because they are limited in the information they have about themselves. They do not know anyone who is like them.

Most of your child's behavior as an adolescent is a means to making an autonomous statement or to finding the real person within. Some adopted youngsters, however, will act out in an effort to test their parents' love. These children are usually filled with profound feelings of inadequacy about their adoption. They believe that they were placed for adoption because they were defective; their bioparents would have kept them if they had been more adequate (see chapter 10). Intellectually, they can accept and understand why a child becomes adoptable, but it is difficult to accept the fact that *they* were placed for adoption. How could their bioparents have rejected them after they saw them? In their fantasies, these children create ways in which their bioparents could have kept them. Then they get angry when they look at what actually happened: They were relinquished for adoption.

If your teenager is suffering through extreme feelings of abandonment and rejection, he or she may try to test your love. Even though they know that you have stuck by them through the years, they may still question whether they are lovable. Make the distinction between your real love for them and whether they believe that they are lovable and worthy. Their actions during these years may result from powerful feelings of worthlessness and inadequacy. When they are able to work through these emotions and come to terms with who they really are, they will begin to view your relationship differently.

Youngsters who were adopted at an early age may deal with feelings of low self-worth in another way. These teenagers may try to retreat from their emotions, not by acting out but by going into seclusion. They will spend prolonged periods of time in their rooms, have few friends, and experience mild to severe depression. It will seem as if they have lost interest in life, and nothing is significant (see "The Suicidal Teenager" on page 132).

All adopted youngsters will experience feelings of low self-esteem and inadequacy at some time during their growing-up years. Adopted teenagers deal with these emotions more profoundly because they are forced to face identity issues during this stage of development. As they get to know themselves and appreciate who they are, they will gradually let go of their old doubts and questions and move into a more realistic appraisal of their assets and liabilities.

Adoptive Parents and Their Feelings

As adoptive parents, you may also feel inadequate during your child's teen years. Your doubts probably started when your child was in puberty and have continued to gnaw away at you. As your youngster acts out extreme behavior, you may question where you went wrong. You will ask yourself whether you should have done one thing or another. Perhaps you should have said "no" when your son wanted to have a friend over and he had not finished his homework. Or, maybe you should have listened to your spouse when your daughter wanted to stay out until 1:00 A.M. If only you . . .

Your child's actions may remind you of your own escapades during your teenage years, and you may become frightened, remembering the risks you had taken at the same age. As a parent, you will try to protect your child from the mistakes you made. And, as a child, your youngster will have to find out for himself.

As your teenagers struggle to find themselves, you will learn to come to terms with the fact that they are getting ready to leave the nest. All parents have to deal with the inevitable breaking-away period, but, as adoptive parents, you may have a harder time adjusting. When your children are teenagers, you will be forced to reminisce about the past. You will remember the "good old days" when your son or daughter hung on your every word, looked to you for guidance, and got involved in only minor scrapes and had problems that had simple solutions.

As you recall those times, you will also go back to the experiences of the period before you had children. The deep hurts left over from your feelings about infertility will return, and you will think again of the time when you had no children and how empty your life was then. You will smile and feel a special warmth as you think about how it felt to hold your child for the first time.

Then, you will come back once more to the present and face a teenager who is ready to leave you and make his or her way in the world.

Many of us have difficulty preparing for the time when our children will be adults. As your teenager continues to act out, you may be reminded more than once of your infertility, and you may believe that you were never meant to have children. You will use your child's behavior as proof that you are poor parents, as if being infertile meant that you did not know how to parent a child.

Some of you will question your decision to adopt. When your teenager thoroughly exasperates you, you may even want to send him away until he becomes human again. All parents feel this way from time to time, but adoptive parents may carry a burden of guilt when they consider that they want their youngsters to leave. You may get angry at yourself for feeling that you want to reject your son or daughter. You may believe that you are ungrateful and do not appreciate the fact that you have a child.

As you continue to berate yourself, your youngster will go about the business of being a "teenager," with all of the attending characteristics. If teenagers become aware of your insecurities, they will use them to try to gain power and control and get their own way. Don't allow your guilty feelings to get in the way of parenting. Your child needs you now more than ever. Your strength and guidance will help the family through this rough period.

Now that you see yourself more realistically, let's look at some specific problems that affect all families with children in the throes of adolescence.

Dealing with Problems

We have already talked about some general guidelines for dealing with issues and problems during the teenage years. There are, however, some specific areas of concern that affect all parents who have teenagers. We know that adolescents will test and act out during these years in an effort to clearly define who they are, and that most adopted teenagers will make a greater statement and experience a more intense period as they come to terms with their identity dilemma. Adolescence is a period of experimentation.

Drugs and Alcohol

Joanne and Dave managed to get through their son Craig's puberty with no major catastrophes. They were disappointed with his grades, but they were looking forward to Craig's high school years as a time to focus on preparing for college.

When Craig was fifteen years old, he began to associate with new friends that Joanne and Dave did not always approve of. Craig, however, always managed to be a part of the family and was generally a "good kid." Joanne and Dave were dumbfound when Craig showed them his first progress report from high school—not at all the "As" and "Bs" they used to see. He needed to improve in all of his classes. Joanne and Dave began to doubt their original perception of Craig's abilities and wondered if they might be expecting too much from him.

Craig had been adopted as an infant, and all through his childhood, Joanne and Dave had tried to set realistic goals for him. They looked for clues from Craig to help them along the way. They thought they knew their child pretty well, until now, that is. Poor grades and questionable friends didn't add up to the child they had always known.

As Joanne and Dave began to assess what was happening, they found other signs that they did not like. They learned that Craig had been tardy and absent from school on many occasions. In addition, Joanne had found money missing from her purse, which she had attributed to her own forgetfulness.

When they first thought that Craig could be involved with drugs, Joanne and Dave dismissed the idea as preposterous—not their family, not their child. But they soon realized that they must confront the problem and needed some help.

As most parents who are facing the possibility that their child is using drugs or alcohol, Joanne and Dave at first denied that there was a problem. They found ways to rationalize Craig's behavior and would not allow themselves to see what was actually happening. When they confronted Craig, he denied his involvement with drugs and temporarily allayed their fears.

As most children who use drugs, Craig believed that he did not have a problem and that his parents just did not understand. They were of a different generation. Smoking pot was something everyone did. When he began to drink beer as well, he felt that he was old enough to handle it and decided that alcohol helped him push away some of his self-doubts. Besides, he had become very popular, something he always yearned for as a young child. Cocaine forced Craig to look at what he was doing to himself. He tried to stop, but he couldn't. Craig was relieved when his parents finally stepped in.

Many families with adolescents share the experiences of Joanne, Dave, and Craig. Joanne and Dave were naive to believe that their child could never get into drugs or alcohol. They did not want to see what was really going on. When they finally confronted the issue, they realized how helpless they had felt and how much they had been avoiding their own feelings by not forcing Craig to face his problem.

Craig went into an inpatient drug program for two months and has since continued to attend regular meetings with his peers. He has been sober and drug free for a year and a half, and now, with the help of additional counseling, is better able to handle his life and to understand himself. The relationship he now has with his parents is better than it ever was, and his grades in school have improved.

You do not have to let drugs or alcohol become a problem in your family. Here are some telltale signs that indicate that your youngster may be using.

If your son or daughter is using drugs or alcohol, you will see changes in their behavior and appearance:

- A drop in grades and loss of interest in school.
- Lack of motivation in school and other activities.
- Poor memory, forgetfulness.
- Lack of interest in personal grooming.
- Change of friends and peer group.
- Loss of appetite, weight loss, pale complexion.
- Sudden mood changes, irritability.
- Low energy, loss of enthusiasm.
- Eyes that are bloodshot and glazed, drooping eyelids.
- Intoxication.

You may also find the actual evidence of drug and alcohol use:

- Marijuana cigarettes, cocaine powder, tablets.
- Plants, leaves, seeds.
- Roach clips, bongs, straws, mirrors.
- Empty beer cans, half-empty bottles of wine, liquor or watered-down liquor.

You may also discover:

- Money is missing.
- Your silver, jewelry, and valuables are disappearing.

If your children are using drugs or alcohol, they will deny it when you confront or question them. Although it is possible that you may not find sufficient evidence to indicate that your kids are involved in alcohol and drugs, a severe change in behavior is certainly a major clue. Don't let your children talk you out of your suspicions. Check them out. Be sure. If you are confused, consult with a professional who can help you make a determination.

Drug use can build. What starts out as one beer or one drag on a marijuana cigarette can escalate into a full-blown cocaine addiction. Drug and alcohol abuse can be stopped early and, as parents, you are the ones who must set the limits with your children. Don't be afraid to take a stand.

Sex and Your Teenager

Sexual awareness and society's attitudes about sex have certainly changed over the years. Teenagers today know more about sex and are probably more sexually experienced than their parents were at the same age. Attitudes, mores, and peer pressure all support sexual relationships between unmarried couples. Adolescents want to know as much as possible about life, and sex is very much a part of it.

As your teenagers begin to understand themselves, they will be better able to set their own realistic limits based on their judgment. Although you may go through some trying moments along the way with your children, your input will always be very important. Teenagers need structure and limits, their parents are the best persons to provide them. Even though the tensions between you and your adolescent are greatest at this time, you must help him or her with your wisdom and guidance.

You can give your teenagers facts about sex, contraception, and sexually transmitted diseases. They need your advice and honest discussion and comments. Speak out. Be open and truthful. Don't let your teenagers struggle with the information they will receive from their peers about sex. They need the facts. Help them sort out what is myth and what is reality.

In addition to the dialogue you will have with your teenagers about sex, give them articles to read and instructional materials and tell them where they can get more information. Your teenagers may be shy when talking to you about sex. It will help them if you are relaxed and not embarrassed. The booklets and articles that you give them to read will also help you. Do not assume that they will comprehend everything they read. Go over the material with them so that you know they understand.

If your youngsters know that you can discuss everything with them, they will not be afraid to talk to you about sex or anything else. You must pave the way; you must set the climate.

Some adoptive parents worry that their children will become sexually active and conceive a child, repeating their bioparents' mistake. If you have this fear, it is important to discuss it openly with your teenager. Listen to their comments. Help them to understand your concern. You may know intellectually that conceiving a child "out of wedlock" is not an inheritable act, but your worries stem from your own experiences as adoptive parents. Your awareness is finely tuned. You know what happens when two people conceive a child that they cannot care for. Keep in mind, though, that your child does not have to repeat the mistakes of his or her bioparents.

After talking to your adolescent, you may find that he or she is also concerned about conceiving a child outside marriage. Some adopted children may have been relinquished from an intact family, but most of them were conceived "out of wedlock." Your youngster may tell you how strongly she feels about giving up a child or having an abortion. Many of them will declare that they would keep their child no matter what. They will believe that somehow they could make it work.

As you listen, you may believe that your children are making statements about their relationship with you, and you may feel slighted and discounted. What they are really talking about is the loss they feel—the loss of their biological heritage. They may not be able to clarify exactly what their emotions are telling them, but if anyone were to ask them about their real parents, they would, without hesitation, refer to you.

If you adopted because of infertility, you may be envious of your adolescent's fertility. He or she possesses something that you had always wanted but could never have. You know how precious life really is, and you may see your teenager taking this gift for granted, just as many individuals do. Perhaps this is the time when you can share with them how you feel about life and birth and how valuable both are to you. Your openness will give your children a deeper understanding of how much they mean to you.

Some theorists have hypothesized that adoptive parents are

very cavalier compared to most parents when it comes to their attitudes about their children and sex. I have never found this to be so. Most adoptive parents are acutely sensitive to the ramifications of their children's sexuality and the possibilities of conceiving a child outside marriage. They want to be sure that their children are thoroughly prepared for both the emotional and physical intimacy of a sexual relationship.

Your children need you to guide them. Let them know about your thoughts and feelings so that they may tell you theirs. Don't let them down.

Prolonged Adolescence

When teenagers are unable to satisfactorily resolve their identity crisis, they may prolong their adolescence for many years. They perpetuate the acting-out phase of the teen years and never grow up. Although there are many biological youngsters who attempt to perpetuate their childhood, adopted children may have a harder time growing up. Their identity confusion can be so profound that they are unable to come to terms with who they really are. Many of them are afraid to face who they might be and may consciously or unconsciously sabotage becoming an adult. Usually at the root of their problem is a fear that if they come to terms with their identity they will find a defective or bad person within themselves. They may believe that they will have nothing to offer society or themselves or that they do not have the wherewithal to be successful, competent adults.

Adoptive parents may collude with their children and not allow them to grow up in an effort to keep them from leaving home. These parents are afraid to feel the loss of and separation from their children. They are usually preoccupied with their roles as parents and are unable to see themselves as separate from their children. Biological parents may also attempt to keep their children close to them, but adoptive parents who have never completely worked through their infertility issues may make it more difficult for their children. All parents who keep their youngsters dependent communicate that they believe their children are ineffective as individuals.

If you are parents who want to hang on to your children, it

is time to do some soul-searching. Help your youngsters become the very best adults they can be. Don't let your own needs get in the way. (We will also discuss children as adults in chapter 12.)

The Suicidal Teenager

Both biological and adoptive families can face the trauma of dealing with children who become deeply depressed during their teen years. Some youngsters may try to tempt fate with extreme risk-taking behavior like racing cars or using drugs and alcohol. Whether depressed or acting out, these youngsters are at a high risk for suicide. They may deliberately choose to end their lives or may do so accidentally.

If you see that your teenager is behaving in an extreme fashion, SEEK HELP IMMEDIATELY. Don't wait for things to get worse or hope that they'll get better or deny that there is a problem. You may be taking chances with your child's life. Get the help your family needs and confront the problem before it's too late.

When You Need to Be Firm

One of the most difficult tasks for all parents is to set limits and structure for their adolescent. Most parents want to be fair and reasonable when they guide their teenager, yet they don't want to be too indulgent. Most children respond well to a sensible approach; however, some will defy you and test the limits, appearing never to learn from past mistakes and making your job as parent almost impossible to carry out.

Adoptive parents seem to have the most difficulty in coming to terms with their own actions when their child's behavior is intolerable. If you are one of these parents, you will not be able to control your youngster because you will be caught up in adoption issues. Whenever you look at your teenagers, you will focus on their feelings of rejection about their adoption and abandonment issues. You will project your own emotions on to your teenagers and believe that you must do nothing to foster the loss they already feel because of their adoption.

As your children's actions become more insufferable, you will remain resolute about doing nothing to remind them of their adoption issues. You will continue to justify your behavior and theirs and hope that they will grow out of it. You may rationalize that your son will change once he is an adult, and you are only giving him the nurturing he so desperately needs.

Then, your teenager will harm another person or himself; he may even commit a crime. By this time you will have set a pattern of indulgence and will accept any action. What can you do?

Let's look for a moment at difficult children. They usually warn their parents early in their development that they are more of a problem than most children. These youngsters require a more structured environment with firm limits. If they are permitted to get away with intolerable behavior at an early age, they will get worse as they get older. By the time they reach their teen years, they will be impossible to live with and relate to.

Let's see how Lois and Rick dealt with their irascible teenage son, Tom.

> Tom was always getting into trouble of one sort or another. Through the years Lois and Rick attempted to handle each situation with a mixture of understanding and caring. They knew that Tom had difficulty dealing with conflicts and did not handle frustration very well.
>
> When Tom turned sixteen years old, things really got out of hand. He would completely defy his parents. He would use their cars without permission, come in at all hours of the night, or, when he did come home early, he would climb out of his window and disappear for hours.
>
> Tom's grades declined, and he was frequently truant and tardy. His appearance was sloppy and unkempt, and his room was a shambles. When Lois and Rick confronted him about his behavior, he assured them that he would try harder. He was very convincing when he talked to them, and they believed that they could trust his intentions.
>
> For two years, Lois and Rick tried to cope with Tom. Tom dropped out of school during that time and had six jobs in one year. Finally, when Tom was eighteen years old, Lois and Rick told him that if he did not go

to school full-time or work steadily, he would have to leave the house. Tom chose to leave.

Lois and Rick had reached their limit with Tom. They anguished for a long time over their decision and worried that Tom might not make it out in the harsh world. Tom struggled for three years, at times barely able to make ends meet. He did maintain some contact with his parents, though, and then one day he asked if he could come home. He was ready to take life seriously and go back to school.

Lois and Rick agreed, but they set down some very strict limits about what they would accept and expect from Tom. It worked. Tom is now in graduate school, studying and striving toward personal goals that he and his family thought he could never attain.

What happened to Lois, Rick, and Tom was the accumulated effect of years of difficulties. Many families with biological children deal with similar issues. Unmanageable children are not unique to adoptive families. The severity of the problems varies from family to family. However, when parents take a firm stand and set strict limits early in their youngster's teen years, they may avoid the more intense issues. As parents, you have a right to expect certain standards from your children in your home. You are obligated to help your children to learn to act responsibly.

Follow these five steps when you need to be firm:

1. Set down the rules clearly and decidedly.
2. Let your teenagers know that you expect no less than what you stated.
3. Spell out the consequences.
4. Be ready to send your adolescents to the home of a relative, friend, or other parent if they are not willing to comply. (There are usually other parents who will be willing to cooperate with you.)
5. Follow through.

Many of you will find it is not easy to be resolute. You may worry that your son or daughter will run away from home if you set limits. Some teenagers may try to run away, but usually wind up spending several days with a close friend. Some adolescents, however, will take greater risks to defy your authority. Just consider the alternatives. Your son or daughter could continue to get into trouble if you do not take a stand.

You may have to put your teenager into a drug rehabilitation program against her will. She may fight you all the way, trying to convince you that she can quit on her own. Decide what is best for you and your family and then do what you have to do. Be part of the process. Follow through. Do not allow your youngster to manipulate you.

When you set firm limits for your children, they may become angry at you, question your love, and tell you that they hate you or that you are not a good parent. Don't get swept up into your own issues of adequacy as parents. Stand firm. Know that you are doing what any responsible parent must do.

Your Teenager's Very Own Adoption Story

During the teenage years, your children will want to know more about their adoption. As they explore themselves and take stock of who they are, they will need to make their adoption story more complete. They may have many more questions about why and how it happened. Their curiosity is based on their complete understanding of the process of adoption. You have already given them a lot of information during puberty; any additional information you may have that can help your youngsters understand more about their adoption should be given to them during adolescence. It will allow them to complete the picture, and you will have another opportunity for dialogue and communication. If you have a picture, letter, or memento that would have meaning to your child, this is the time to give it to him or her.

If your teenager does not ask you about her adoption, tell her that you have more facts for her if she is interested. Then wait. Don't push. She will need time. She wants to know, yet she is afraid. Several years may go by before she is ready, but she will remember your dialogue with her and reach out to you when she is able to hear more.

When You Adopt a Teenager

Puberty and adolescence are the most trying periods for the adoptive family. Both parents and children confront adoption more realistically than they have ever done before. Each assesses and reappraises self and others, looking for answers and hoping for solutions and resolution. Children who are adopted as teenagers will have a very difficult adjustment and may never be able to form a bond of attachment to the adoptive parents. If you adopt a teenager, your youngster's past attachments will affect the nature of the relationship he or she will have with you. As your teenager attempts to form a new relationship with you, he must also deal with the developmental issues of separating and becoming an independent individual. His biological timetable tells him to break away, to separate.

At the same time, these teenagers must come to terms with their anger about the past and may be locked in conflict over it. You and other people may become the objects of their frustration. They may act out in destructive ways when they are unable to come to terms with what has happened to them in the past. Many of these youngsters have lived in orphanages or have been shifted to and from various foster homes during their lifetime.

Counseling or therapy may help you and your newly adopted adolescent. During the process, you will learn to respect one another, and your teenager will be able to understand the inner turmoil and the powerful feelings that motivate her. Once your teenager works through those emotions, she can view you and herself more realistically. The process is usually long and slow but potentially effective.

As adoptive parents, you have now completed all the years of development with your child. Your relationship has evolved and now you are ready to move on into an adult relationship.

12

All Grown Up

"Will my parents ever stop treating me like a child?"

Barbara, twenty-seven years old, had lived with her parents from the time she was adopted in infancy until the age of twenty-two, when she moved into her own apartment after landing a promotion in the marketing firm where she was working. She had recently been offered an opportunity for further advancement in her career, which would mean a great deal of travel. Her parents expressed concern for her safety, which led to an argument.

Barbara was frustrated about her relationship with her parents. Even though she had been living away from her family home for several years, her parents were always attempting to direct her life. Although Barbara was able to handle her parents' intrusion, she never liked it.

Now, as much as Barbara tried to explain her position, her parents still attempted to persuade her to reject the job offer. The discussions escalated into anger and, finally, to no communication at all.

When Barbara accepted the new position, she did so with a great deal of guilt and felt frustrated by her parents' lack of support for her success.

Barbara's story is not very different from that of other adult children, whether adopted or not. As children become adults, their parents are not always ready to accept the growth and changes that occur. Some parents do not believe that their children can create their own lives and take full responsibility for themselves and want to prevent them from making mistakes or being hurt.

Moreover, overprotective parents want to shield themselves from the loss that they will feel if they allow their children to grow up. They may not have effectively prepared themselves during the teenage years and are now holding on for dear life. In an attempt not to feel the loneliness, they are desperately trying to retain the old parent-child relationship.

If you cling to your children long after they have become adults, you are avoiding and denying your own feelings about separation and loss. YOUR CHILDREN WILL GROW UP AND BECOME ADULTS IN SPITE OF YOUR EFFORTS, so you might as well accept the inevitable and learn how to make your son's or daughter's adulthood a positive experience for all.

Hanging On—Letting Go

Your adult children will be pulling away from you even as you strive to delay their maturing. Even though they want to go out on their own, they will have many doubts about their ability to do so. This tug-of-war serves to reinforce your child's uncertainties and guilt. The unspoken message from you is "You really can't make it. You still need *Mommy* and *Daddy.*"

It will not be easy to let go of the old parent-child relationship. Both you and your child will shift back and forth until you find just the right balance. Your child's ambivalence about growing up and leaving home may be a theme for some time before he or she actually makes the final break. This period does not have to be a great struggle if you know what to expect and are prepared.

When your children become adults, you will experience another period of trial and error. Your children will not go to sleep one day as youngsters and wake up the next as adults. Their desire to grow up will be a very powerful force in their lives, and you will watch them as if they are driven, compelled to make separate lives for themselves. They will question every step of the way with you. If you hold on, you will add to their fears about leaving home.

Some of your children will be ready to leave when they are eighteen years old without much of a struggle at all. Others may move out only to return after many months or even a year or two. Your children may even remain at home indefinitely, finding excuses that force them to stay with you. At first, you may welcome the opportunity to extend your parenting role, but may then find that you have perpetuated their childhood, not allowing yourselves to have lives of your own or helping them find the courage to leave.

Both you and your adult child will be confused during the early adult years. As your child tries to find a life path, you will redefine your position in all of this.

As you prepare for your child's adulthood:

- Consider that he is ready to move on.
- Know that her inner drives and biological and social timetables are pushing her forward.
- Understand that he is eager to plan his life, to set new directions.
- Believe in her need to test her strengths and limitations further.
- Remember that he is both excited and afraid.

Before we talk further about your role in your adult child's life, let's look at adulthood and what it means for all families.

Full Bloom

In many ways, adult adoptees are just like all other adults. They will move through the same stages of adulthood: young adults, mature individuals, and finally, seniors. Each life stage will create predictable events along the way, and your adopted child will travel the path of adulthood with every other adult.

What seems to be lacking today for most adults is the absence of rituals or ceremonies to mark the occasion of adulthood. In the past, children would leave home at the time of their marriage, and the wedding ceremony would serve as the rite of passage into adulthood. Today, many individuals move out of their parents' home and live on their own for years before marrying. In addition, many couples choose to live together before marriage and some have decided not to marry at all.

As a young adult, your child will make decisions about career, lifestyle, and friends. Dreams shaped when they were in their twenties will be reevaluated at mid-life. Your adult child will move on in his or her life, just as you and others before you did, and just as future generations will do. You hope that when your adult children enter their senior years they will have had some personal happiness and have reached a stage of contentment and satisfaction that will carry them for the remainder of their lives.

Your adult children will experience crises just as you did. They will learn from their mistakes, perhaps making the same mistakes, and continue to grow and change. You will watch with pleasure and, sometimes, disappointment, knowing that you have done all that you could do, and it is time for your son or daughter to lead his or her own life.

The Process: Painful or Positive?

At a workshop I attended several years ago, the leader was helping a mother and adult daughter change their relationship from parent-child to friends. Both women were asked to stand up and face each other, embrace, and then repeat these words:

SUSAN (daughter):   "Good-bye, mother."
                                     "Hello, Ann."
                                     "I'm Susan."
ANN (mother):   "Good-bye, daughter."
                                     "Hello, Susan."
                                     "I'm Ann."

At first, it was very difficult for the women to complete the exercise. They tripped over some of the words and had to begin over again. With a great deal of concentration, they were finally able to do it. As they practiced, it became easier. They were overcoming old established patterns that were hard to break. Once they were able to say the simple words with ease, they realized that the relationship had already changed, and they were beginning a new friendship.

Without the clear-cut rituals to mark new roles and responsibilities between parents and their children, it becomes even more necessary for you as parents to consciously plan for your independence and that of your children. Make the next stage a happy, secure, and stable one with greater flexibility, tolerance, and respect for one another.

When an adoptee becomes an adult, you will react according to your own life adjustments and experiences. Those of you who are ready to move on into your own appropriate stage of life will easily accept your adult child's need to separate, and you will help him or her do so. You will see your son or daughter as an adult, and you will accept and respect that. Your friendship will grow as you let go of the old parent-child relationship. You will become valued friend to your adult child, and he or she will provide a special kind of friendship to you.

As you look at and relate to your adult child, you will see a separate person with a unique appearance, abilities, and limitations. All parents will need to view their adult children as separate and unique, and adoptive parents will become acutely aware of how important heredity is as a factor in personal identity. Those of you who have photographs of your child's bioparents will see the strong physical resemblance between your child and them. You will also be confronted with the final reality of the differences between you and your child. If you have clung to the fantasies that your son or daughter could be like you, you can no longer perpetuate the myth. You must abandon these unrealistic expectations and illusions once and for all. Your children were great youngsters and they can be even greater adults if you let them be the individuals they need to be.

If you continue to deny the disparities between you, separation could become a major crisis for your family. You may try to keep your children with you in order to control their lives or to make them into the individuals you had always wanted them to be. Some parents attempt to hold on in an effort to avoid feelings of loneliness. When you take your child's need to separate personally, you help to sustain the fear and guilt that your son or daughter may already feel. Adoptees, like all children, know when their actions disturb their parents. They don't want to consciously hurt you, yet they may believe that they must placate you in order to move on with their lives. Resentments will build as your child tries to go ahead and still play the role of your youngster. The problem is that they cannot be truthful with you. They sense that their honesty will hurt you and will alienate them from you even though they love you and need you. Their dilemma can be solved only if you accept their needs and desires.

YOU CAN BE SUPPORTIVE AND STILL LET GO.

You will have problems when your child becomes an adult if the communication between you has been stifled. Most adult children who experience alienation from their families are usually unable to have any dialogue with them. Many times, these patterns are established early in their childhood and continue into the adult years. Your relationship with your adult child must be based on open dialogue and communication to survive. It is never too late to start talking; in fact, it is vital to your relationship as adults and as friends.

YOU CAN CHANGE THE PATTERNS.

As you listen to what your adult son or daughter has to tell you, you will be confronted with more statements about his or her individuality.

This is a chance to:

- Look at these adults who also happen to be your children.
- Learn more about them.
- Accept and respect who they are.
- Hear what they have to say.
- Allow them to give you some of their wisdom.
- Be open to a lifelong friendship.

One of the most difficult tasks for you or any parent is to accept your son's or daughter's life choices when they are different from your own. It is unlikely that your child will change very much from the person he or she has become. What you see now, except for some minor modifications and adjustments, is the child you raised, whom you deeply love, and who loves you in return. The emotional bond that was formed when you first looked at your son or daughter as an infant or a youngster only deepens as he or she becomes an adult.

YOU CAN VALUE YOUR ADULT CHILDREN.

Your adult children may decide on careers or jobs that are very different from yours, or they may struggle with life commitments and decisions for a long time. They may go on to college and seek a profession, or they may get a job right out of high school and not continue their education. Their choices may be difficult or easy for them to make. As parents, you will want to come to their assistance, to make the choice less burdensome, but in the long run, you will only be prolonging their inevitable determination. Your role is to give them emotional support and guidance, to allow them to struggle, but not to perpetuate their childhood. It will be easy for them to lean heavily on you if you let them. The ultimate goal is for them to break out on their own.

YOU CAN HELP YOUR ADULT CHILDREN STAY FOCUSED.

Let them know that it is appropriate to:

• Be confused during young adulthood.
• Be afraid to make life choices.
• Want to remain protected.
• Have doubts about themselves and their decisions.

Help them by:

• Listening.
• Showing them their options.
• Telling them that they can be afraid and still move ahead.
• Letting them know that they can have doubts about their abilities and still move ahead.

- Gradually weaning your financial support.
- Assisting them in finding a place of their own.
- Knowing that they must do a great deal by themselves.
- Allowing you and your spouse to get on with the next stage of your lives.

So You're the Person I Married

The children you raised are finally adults. They are out on their own, doing their own thing, struggling, making mistakes, testing their strengths, creating their lives, working toward fulfillment and contentment. Now you and your spouse can begin a new time in your lives. It may be hard for you to change gears at first, or you may get right on with things. This is an occasion for you and your spouse. You can set new goals or resume pursuits that had been set aside earlier in life. This is a time of opportunity and new possibilities.

You may need to get to know your spouse again. Many couples lose sight of each other during their children's teen years and need to use this period for renewal and restoration. You can consider your relationship as husband and wife without family interferences. This is a time for new understandings and intimacy. Many couples describe these years as the best in their marriage. With changes in responsibilities and more leisure time, they are able to experience a fulfilling marriage, more meaningful than ever before.

Both adoptive and biological parents experience a similar process when their children grow up. Some of you may find that factors get in the way of developing a more satisfying relationship with your spouse. As you take a good look at your husband or wife, you may find a stranger staring back at you. The person you thought you once knew may no longer be there. Instead, you see a new individual you will have to get to know. Your lives have been so focused on careers and children that you have had little time for each other.

And now, here you are, face to face.

Some of you may be able to work through this crisis on your own; others will need help. Don't wait too long to get the help you need. Marriage counselors can help you reestablish goals and make your marriage work again. Consider this time, whether in counseling or not, as an opportunity to have the very best relationship possible, one in which you can grow old with your spouse as companions, lovers, and friends.

The Single Parent

As a single adoptive parent, you may have greater difficulty in letting your son or daughter grow up and become an adult. Most single parents face the end of their child-rearing years as a time of profound separation and loss. Your children must break away, and you must help them make that transition. They will also feel a substantial loss when they leave home and face the world, and they will experience a deep sense of guilt, knowing that they are leaving you alone.

Your role is the same as that of all parents. *You must let your children separate and move on.* It helps if you have other important relationships in your life and a career or other interests that require your attention and provide you with a sense of accomplishment and fulfillment. Once you let go, you will leave yourself open to a new relationship with your adult child. You will still need each other, but now you can be friends.

The Adoption Story Continues

As you observe and relate to your adult child, you will see a separate individual whose appearance, abilities, and limitations are unique. The part heredity played in forming your child's personal identity will be obvious to you now. Of course, you will have had a great influence on your son or daughter, but you will clearly see how heredity and environment worked together to create the adult.

Infertility May Rear Its Head Again

You still may continue to deny those obvious differences between you and your adult children. Through your unwillingness to accept the reality that your children will never be like you, their separation from you may become a major crisis for your family. Some of you may attempt to hold on to your adult children in an effort to avoid your own feelings of loneliness. Unlike other parents who face a sense of emptiness when their children go out on their own, you may also be reminded of your infertility and the time when you had no children and wanted them so desperately. In the past, you were able to avoid the emotions that had consumed you before you had children, but when your child is ready to leave or has already left you to make his own way in the world, you may be confronted with the old pangs of being childless.

You may experience these feelings again when your son or daughter marries and has a baby. As you watch your child antici- pate the arrival of his or her own infant, you might feel a tinge of resentment and envy your child's fertility. You have the choice of joining in the excitement or grieving your loss again. After all, you did have children and were able to reap the joys of parenthood. Now you will have the opportunity to join in the celebration of a new baby in the family. There will be new rewards for you as grandparents. So join in the special occasion.

I was fortunate to be part of the process when my adopted daughter gave birth to her daughter. During the hours in the labor room with her I felt a connection to her that I had never experienced before. It was as if she were being born all over again and *I* was giving birth to *her.* The specialness of that event will always be a part of me.

Adult Adoptees

As adults, adoptees deal with all of the problems that most adults face during the various stages of life and encounter many other issues as well. Their unique needs as adoptees may be even more significant during adulthood. This is the time when they must take all of the information they know about them- selves and make it work for them.

WHAT DO THEY ACTUALLY KNOW?

They can look in the mirror and see an image before them. Their experiences thus far have told them a little more. They may have some sketchy background material that was given to you at the time they were adopted—that's all they have. There are many unknowns, voids, and unanswered questions. As they embark on the journey of life, they are lone travelers with partially full suitcases.

WHAT DO THEY HAVE IN COMMON WITH OTHER ADOPTEES?

Many adoptees have difficulty with separation and may hang on to relationships because "good-byes" are difficult for them. They seem to project their own feelings about being abandoned and rejected onto everyone else; they can't let go. At times, they believe that if they move away from a relationship, even if this friendship is not in their best interests, they will never make new friends. These feelings may extend to their parents, and they may not be able to leave home at an appropriate time.

Some adoptees are afraid to try new life experiences, holding back instead of forging ahead. Others describe themselves as being impulsive about decisions, having a low tolerance for frustration. They want everything to happen right away and can't wait for tomorrow. As they attempt to make life decisions, they can be severely critical of themselves and experience a diminished self-esteem as they plan their lives. Many times they feel like outsiders, different from everyone else, with a sense of detachment and rootlessness. As they struggle with the need to experience a biological connection, they may marry at an early age and have children to fill the void they feel.

Some female adoptees may become pregnant before they are married in an effort to undo what their bioparents did. These wishes are often unconscious, and these women are not even aware of their intentions until they are faced with giving birth. They strongly believe that they would never give up their child, no matter what. An abortion is out of the question; after all, they would not have been born if their biomother had decided to terminate her pregnancy.

The conflicts that most adoptees feel about their lack of roots keep them bound to and dependent on the family; however, what they really want most of all is the freedom to make life choices. Instead, many adult adoptees feel as if they can never break free; they remain stuck in childhood. The fear of the unknown seems to be greater than the expectation and anticipation of the future. For a time, adult adoptees may be immobilized by these feelings.

Some adoptees believe that society continues to treat them as children who must be protected from knowing about their biological heritage. They feel stifled and cheated by not knowing as much as everyone else does about their background (see chapter 13).

WHAT DO THEY NEED?

Many adult adoptees are eventually able to break free. It is easier for those who are able to talk about their feelings and frustrations. The greatest conflicts and problems arise when communication has been stifled. Many adoptees, even as adults, believe that they will hurt their parents if they discuss their feelings about being adopted. It is up to you to assure your children that you will not be destroyed or devastated by their honesty and that you are ready, willing, and able to listen to and support them, no matter how they feel.

You can help to support them by:

• Telling them that you understand.
• Allowing them to be frustrated.
• Letting them talk about their feelings.
• Knowing that they may need some extra time to grow up.
• Expressing *your* feelings about what is happening.
• Giving them guidance when they need it.
• Pulling back when they need to struggle.
• Loving them as you always have.

Some adult adoptees are able to move ahead in their lives. With sheer perseverance and tenacity, they can make anything happen. Others are able to get additional information about their biological heritage, which allows them to go forward. Others ultimately search for and have a reunion with their bioparents (see chapter 13). The adoptee's individual style of dealing with all of life's issues will dictate how he or she will handle the adoption issue. As adults, they will finally be able to come to terms with their adoption; somehow they are able to find answers for themselves.

Both you and your adult child will feel more successful if you are open to facing and understanding the unique needs of the adoptive family. You can create rewarding experiences through honest communication in which you explore your emotions with your child. It should be easy at this point—you've already had a great deal of practice.

13

Who Am I?
The Lifelong Quest

An individual's search for identity begins in infancy and is redefined and adjusted in an ongoing process throughout a lifetime. Some people eventually reach an inner peace about who they are; others live in perpetual turmoil, never finding out who they really are. Some attempt to deny their identity, masking it with an outward facade, living a life of pretense in their desire to be someone else.

Identity carries with it a sense of wholeness, a feeling of being complete. When we consider a person's identity, we look at the unity of a multitude of elements that create a oneness, an individuality. More specifically, an identity defines a person as separate and different from all other persons—a unique entity, a separate self not at all like anyone else.

As you watched your infant kick and coo in his crib, you began to see your child's personality emerge. You learned from her that she is very different from you and, as you watched her play with other children, you became even more aware of her uniqueness. As your children grow, you see how they act and react in special ways as they learn about themselves and their world and their relationship to it. Biological children can be seen in the same way. No two individuals are exactly the same, whether or not they are related biologically.

How Identity Is Formed

I can vividly remember the time when one of my sons was ten months old. I heard a loud bang in his room and ran to him. The side of the crib was on the floor, and my son was seated in the corner of the crib with a look of satisfaction on his face. He had managed to unscrew the springs on the crib side and remove them. Astonished, I realized that this behavior was an expression of his unique self that would emerge more during his growing years.

A person's search for identity actually begins at birth. I am sure that you can remember a time early in your child's life when he or she began to display uniqueness. The testing and questioning through nonverbal communication is part of a child's first attempts to find his or her own individuality. Infants begin the steps to putting together their own self-identity puzzle. And, most of the time, parents will only be able to watch in awe.

The formation of a person's identity is usually trial and error—a testing of abilities and limitations, reality and fantasy. Your children will prepare themselves for the discovery of their own identities. They will take you on their journey, uncovering clues along the way that will help them learn more about themselves. As a parent, you will watch and wait for them to complete the voyage and reach the place of knowing themselves. Each person's course varies, but the final goal is the same for everyone: an inner sense of wholeness, contentment, and unity.

Although the search for identity is a lifelong continuous process, several points in time are more significant than others. These are stages when the emergence of self becomes a prevalent theme. The struggles and conflicts of first the toddler and then the teenager are critical identity periods for all individuals.

As adults, your children will experience crises in their lives that will have a substantial impact on their identity. Each change or milestone will create additional opportunities for growth and self-understanding. And your children will respond accordingly.

You, as parents, help your children evaluate themselves in terms of their own identity. As parents, you continuously attempt to validate your children, letting them know that it is essential to be different from you in order to find themselves. By allowing them to explore all possibilities, you will help them do this. Their basic sense of self is formed from many sources, but you are the primary influence. (We have already discussed how heredity and peer relationships play a part in identity formation in chapter 9.)

When you consider how an individual's identity is formed, keep in mind that everyone:

- Has internal drives that push him or her to become a separate person.
- Experiences identity confusion at various times in his or her life.
- Searches for an identity.
- Attempts to resolve identity confusion.

As you try to help your children find themselves, remember:
THE SEARCH FOR AN IDENTITY CAN BE A LIFELONG QUEST.

Struggles and uncertainties about finding oneself are not always part of the process. Many times the path of discovering an identity can be exciting and awesome. Let's find out how adoptees feel about all of this.

The Adoptee

Many adoptees have told me that although they deeply love their adoptive parents and families and have a strong emotional connection to them, they never really experienced a complete affinity. There was always a missing link, a piece that didn't fit. There were times when they felt like bystanders looking in from the outside.

Adoptees who are very different from their families experience a sense of isolation from time to time. They rarely question the love they feel for their parents or the love they receive in return; they are concerned only with their uniqueness within the family. The situations that make them feel most remote are usually those that draw most biological families close together:

family reunions, get-togethers, birthday parties. Adoptees often stand apart at these occasions, feeling shy and alone. A young child may look around the room, searching for someone who resembles him.

A person's identity is formed in a supportive and loving environment and grows out of an identification with the parent of the same sex. This process begins early in every person's life and becomes most significant at the onset of puberty. When the disparities are very great between fathers and sons and mothers and daughters, it is more difficult to form a sense of identity, but not impossible. At times the unknowns and the differences are intolerable for adoptees, and the frustrations may deepen as they attempt to form an identity. Although it is possible to find one's own self without being able to identify with a parent of the same sex, it is not always an easy process. Biological children who grow up in single-parent families have similar difficulties.

Some adult adoptees I've spoken with ask themselves questions like these: "I'm all grown up, but who am I? Where did I come from?" When they were young children, they expected their parents to know everything. They saw their parents as strong, the very foundation of their lives. They expected answers to every question about their background, and believed that their parents could lead them toward an understanding of themselves. When their mothers and fathers were unable to supply these solutions, they became outraged.

As time went on, many of these adoptees and their parents were left with overwhelming feelings of uncertainty. Despite the fact that many adoptive families did have information about their child's biological heritage, it seemed as if it were never enough for many adoptees. If there were few facts available, some adoptees believed that their parents knew more but were not telling. Carried over from their childhood was the myth that their parents should know everything.

With each birthday celebration, some adoptees find that their outrage about not knowing their biological roots increases and, in some cases, becomes unendurable. They are compelled to have more facts to finish the puzzle and firmly believe that they have a right to know. This natural curiosity about ancestry is common to everyone. Some individuals are passionate about their needs; others will only wonder about it as they move on in their lives. A great deal depends on individual temperament and personal style of relating to the world.

Adoptees are thrust into the adult world with limited information about themselves. What they have already learned through their experience will be part of what they need to know; nevertheless, they will move ahead, sometimes with determination, sometimes with caution. Many believe that they are the only ones faced with missing pieces about themselves, and they are the only ones who have to deal with identity issues. It is difficult for them to view themselves as being like everyone else in this respect. They certainly have many more unknowns in their biological heritage, but the need to develop an identity is fundamental to being a human being. *Everyone* deals with identity as a major life issue.

Along with the need to know more is an ambivalence about actually finding out. Adoptees feel compelled to have facts, but are afraid of what they might learn. This push-pull can immobilize many adult adoptees and prevent them from making life decisions. These individuals lose sight of what they already know about themselves and can only focus on the lack of information about their roots. They may feel helpless, inadequate, unable to move ahead, and may refuse to see their assets. While they remain motionless, they avoid the risks of venturing out on their own to create a life for themselves. Therapy could help them to break through these self-imposed barriers. In a therapeutic setting, they will regain or develop their sense of self-worth and move forward toward personal accomplishment and confidence.

Adoptees deserve to feel good about themselves. Before we continue our look at the adoptee's search for identity, let's discuss what we know is true for all adoptees.

All adoptees:

- Have internal drives pushing them to become separate individuals.
- Experience an identity confusion.
- Will search for their own identity.
- Have a natural curiosity about their biological roots.

•Are given little information about their genetic heritage.
•Feel different from their adoptive families.

Some adoptees are compelled to find more answers, to seek out the truth about their genetic heritage. Adoptees have no knowledge of information that everyone else takes for granted and must either come to terms with not knowing or search for the truth.

The Need to Know More . . . the Search

Some adult adoptees seek additional information about their roots. Others are content with what they do know and have no desire to search. Those who search may need to know more about themselves in order to attempt to resolve their identity confusion. When they finally do decide to embark on the unknown journey, it is usually after much inner turmoil and ambivalence. They will proceed with caution and a fear of the unknown.

Adult adoptees are no different from other adoptees. Their need to gain more facts about themselves will be based on their individuality and will have nothing to do with their relationship with you. You have been loving and supportive parents, and your method of parenting or their feelings about you have nothing to do with their search needs. They are responding to internal drives and innate styles of relating to everything, not just adoption.

If your adult children want more information, they may choose to get nonidentifying facts from local or state agencies. Others may not be content with these records and will want to conduct a full-scale search for their biofamilies. Whatever your children decide to do is based on who they are and not on what you did or did not do as parents. Adoptees actively search for information or people when they need to fill in the gaps about themselves.

ADOPTEES ARE NOT LOOKING FOR ANOTHER SET OF PARENTS.
They already have parents: YOU. You will always be your children's parents. Nothing can change that fact.

ADOPTEES ARE NOT LOOKING FOR ANOTHER MOTHER OR FATHER.

They already have a mother or father: YOU.

YOU ARE THE TRUE PARENTS OF YOUR ADOPTED SON OR DAUGHTER.

No one can take that relationship away from you.

I Only Want Medical Information

Sybil had a strong desire to learn more about her background. She wrote to her state agency to get additional information, and when she received the computer printout, she was excited about having facts for the blanks she had carried around all of her life.

The three-page document that she now had in her possession gave her additional medical information that she had always wanted. She had been tired of writing the word *unknown* every time she completed a medical history form at a doctor's office. Now she could fill in some of the spaces.

Sybil was fortunate to get the medical data that she wanted. Many adoptees are not so lucky because a detailed medical history is not usually part of the record. Health information is provided by the bioparents at the time the final adoption papers are signed. The adoption worker asks the bioparents for a health history, but many times the bioparents know very little or make only general statements about the information they do have. The questions posed at the time the papers are signed are usually not specific, and the bioparents are not always encouraged to expand on any information they do have.

I Want to Meet My Bioparents

Only a small percentage of adult adoptees choose to search for their bioparents. When they do, they are usually between twenty-five and thirty-five years of age. It is during this age range that most adults are ready to reach a final resolution of their identity questions. Adults who are older than thirty-five may also choose to search but it does not occur as often. Most infrequently, searches take place when an adoptee is between eighteen- and twenty-five-years old. Search organizations like ALMA (Adoptees' Liberty Movement Association) accept as members only adults who are eighteen years old or older. (See appendix B, "Support Organizations," for additional information.) In my work with adoptees, I have found that the "search" is often precipitated by a major life event such as marriage, pregnancy or the birth of a child, or the death of an adoptive parent.

Adoptees are generally looking for concrete information to help create a stability in their lives. They are not necessarily seeking a relationship with their bioparents. Lasting friendships between siblings is more common. What adoptees want most is to find someone who looks like them. They crave to resemble somebody. Many of them have spent their lives looking for their face in a crowd or on television or at the front door. They dream of being found by someone who looks just like them. When they see a famous person, they fantasize that this individual might be their bioparent.

Adoptees are also seeking validation of their own talents and abilities through a meeting with a bioparent.

Dave had always wanted to be an actor. As a child, he was always pretending, donning a bizarre hat or making up shows to perform for his parents and their friends.

His adoptive parents, who were both teachers, had difficulty understanding Dave's needs and desires. Nevertheless, he became an actor and performed several successful roles onstage. Despite his success, he always had gnawing doubts about his career choice.

When he was thirty-two years old, he decided to seek information about his roots. He contacted the county adoption agency that had handled his adoption, and during a meeting with an adoption worker, he was given nonidentifying information about his bioparents. He learned that they were both actors.

Dave's new knowledge spurred him on to find his biomother and, ultimately, his biofather. When he fi-

nally did meet them, he was thirty-six years old, but
what he saw were two people whom he greatly resem-
bled, not only in appearance but also in personality.

Dave corresponds with his biofather and sees his
biomother from time to time. More important, he has
since achieved new heights in his career.

Dave's experience was one of many possibilities. He was fortunate to turn his fantasies into realities and make some of the
unknowns known. He could now go on with his life with a strong
sense of identity, which he confirmed through his search and
ultimate meeting with his bioparents. The relationship that
formed between them was secondary to his need for validation.
Dave was also lucky to have adoptive parents who helped and
supported him during and after his search efforts.

Not all search experiences turn out the way Dave's did. There
are times when an actual meeting never comes about—when
bioparents cannot be found or have died or refuse to meet with
their biochildren. Sometimes the adoptee has a change of heart
and stops in the middle of the process. In other situations, the
meeting may be a one-time event because the bioparents do not
want to continue a relationship or the adoptee has chosen not
to have one. The meetings can be positive or negative events.
Major disappointments may also be part of the process, but no
matter what occurs, adoptees are finally able to put their fantasies to rest and to confront reality.

The Journey

Search may not be the choice for all adoptees. It will not
answer all questions or solve all problems; it is not a fairy tale
or a panacea. The search journey must be embarked on with
forethought and circumspection. Adoptees must determine
their motives for a search and think about what they expect to
find at the end of the road. Unrealistic expectations should be
discarded in favor of real possibilities. Search groups can lend
support during the process. Within a group, adoptees can learn
from others to know what to expect and how to make it happen.
(See appendix B for search support organizations.)

In addition, working with a therapist who has had experience with search and reunion issues can help to clarify the impact of the process on the adoptive family. Search will profoundly affect the whole family. It is not something to be taken cavalierly; careful planning is necessary so that the optimum benefit is gained from the experience. Whenever possible, adoptive parents should be available to lend support to their children.

Steps Along the Way

The search experience is usually not a direct path from beginning to end; often it is filled with mountains and valleys along the way. Sometimes the road is filled with hurdles and may even be a dead end. Although each search experience is unique, with its own beginning, middle, and end, all searches have many aspects in common.

All adoptees who want to search will almost always begin with a need to have more factual information, but they do not necessarily feel compelled to do anything about it. Some are outraged that the data are not readily available, but, at first, they will merely complain about the lack of information. It may take many months or even years until the actual information is sought.

After the additional facts are obtained, the adoptee is satisfied for a while; however, this complacency does not always last. An obsession takes over, and the adoptee is not satisfied until all of the answers are found:

SEARCH BECOMES A COMPULSIVE MISSION.

For those adoptees who go through the process of search, their adoptive parents are also part of the process. What role can adoptive parents play when their children search for their identity and biological roots?

The Role of Adoptive Parents

Many adoptive parents can only stand by helplessly as they watch their children struggle with identity issues. Even though these parents want to help, their input is usually inadequate and falls short of what is needed. I remember telling my own children that I did not have the answers for them, but if they still wanted to know more when they were adults, I would help them search for more information. I made that statement many times without knowing if I could get the answers for them.

Some of you may have met your children's bioparents and do have additional facts that could be helpful. Others will not be able to fill in the gaps because you do not have a lot of data. Remember, not even a complete biological history may be enough for some adoptees.

Your children, like all adoptees, will have a natural curiosity about their roots. Their inquisitiveness will begin during childhood, and their style of pursuing solutions to problems and unknowns will be unique. By the time they reach adulthood, you will know them well and have a clear understanding of their individual personality. You will have learned the give-and-take of your relationship, and, most importantly, a bond of love will have grown between you through nurturing, caring, and mutual respect.

It is important to note here that most people have a natural curiosity about their heritage and roots; they like to know about their genealogy and their ancestors. Unlike adoptees, biological children have opportunities throughout their lives to get first-hand knowledge through living relatives, who are usually only too happy to talk about the past. Verbal histories are part of most families.

Whether your children choose to simply seek additional information or embark on a full-fledged search for their bioparents, you may feel somewhat threatened. As adoptive parents, you have dealt with questions throughout your child's life. His or her adoption was a topic that you discussed freely. But when your youngster asked you to repeat his own adoption story or your teenager asked for more facts, you might have felt slightly wary about the status of your relationship with your child. Did you wonder if you could have done something that day to make you less of a parent and to prompt your child's focus on adoption? Then you would push away your doubts and believe in yourself again.

Parents who have adopted several children also fear that if one child is more curious than the others, he or she may influence the others to search for more information. Although siblings do have a great deal of impact on one another, much of what each child thinks, feels, and does depends greatly on that child's own individuality, style, and personality. No child can convince another to do something that he or she does not wish to do. Your children will have independent thoughts and feelings about their own adoption. All adoptees share certain universal truths about adoption, but each adoptee has a unique way of dealing with these truths. Your children's choice to search or not stems from who they are and has little to do with their environment.

At one time or another, all adoptive parents feel threatened when their children ask questions about adoption. Usually, these moments are short-lived and pass quickly. Occasionally, a television special or news article acts as a threat. There have been many stories in the media about adoptees' reunions with their biofamilies. These occasions are always portrayed as happy events that usually do not include the adoptive parents. It is understandable that you might feel intimidated after viewing such an incident.

When my children were young, I returned home from my office early one evening to find them sprawled on the floor in front of the television, watching one of their favorite programs. In that particular segment, a young woman was trying to find her bioparent. She had been adopted in infancy, and she decided to search when her adoptive parents died.

I felt a sense of panic come over me. My children are too young and impressionable to watch this, I thought. It will put ideas in their heads. I toyed with the notion of shutting off the television set. Instead, I watched along with them, caught up in the story. When the young woman finally met her biomother, I felt a pang of outrage.

And then I cried. Tears just rolled down my cheeks. Thoughts ran through my mind as I became more and more swept up in the program: How dare you take her from me! I'm her real mother. I changed her dirty diapers, stayed up with her at night, taught her how to tie her shoelaces. I won't let you have her!

I composed myself at the end of the show and said "good night" to my children. I asked them how they felt about the program. They said it was OK, kissed me, and went to bed. For a long time I sat in my chair, stunned by my reaction to what I had seen. I was supposed to be beyond all of those feelings. After all, I was perfectly secure in my relationship with my daughter and sons. I knew that no one could take them away from me.

Years later, when I talked more openly with my children about the program, they indicated that they did not even remember the segment. Evidently it did not have the same impact on them as it did on me. I know that my emotions were part of being a parent of very young children and wanting so much to protect that relationship. Now, that emotional bond has grown and matured into a lasting friendship of love that can never be taken away.

If my children do search and have reunions with their biofamilies, that meeting and possible relationship will have little bearing on the relationship we have established over the years. One of my children is considering a search, and I know that I will be there to help in whatever way I can.

Janet was not as sure of her relationship with her daughter, Doreen.

> When Doreen first came in to see me, she was thirty-six years old, married, and the mother of one son. She was preparing to write to the state of California for additional data concerning her adoption. Although her parents had given her some information, Doreen believed she needed more.
>
> Doreen appeared fidgety and continuously apologized for her need to have answers. She said that although her husband was supportive of her plan, her parents knew nothing of what she was doing. Even though she would like to conduct a full-scale search for her bioparents, she believed that if she did, she would betray her parents, whom she dearly loved and with whom she was very close.
>
> After many months, Doreen received the computer printout from Sacramento but was still not satisfied. She decided that the only way to put her curiosity to rest would be to search. Each time she contemplated

the possibility, she would think of her mother and how difficult it would be for her to accept the plan. Yet, Doreen knew that she needed her mother's support to complete the mission.

Doreen was also concerned that a search for her bioparents would destroy the relationship she had with her parents, in particular, her mother. Her conflict and turmoil plagued her until finally one day she decided she would break the news to her parents. She set up a day when they could be close and have enough time to talk about what would happen and how it would take place. More important, Doreen wanted her parents to know how much she loved and needed them and how much she wanted them to support her during the search.

Doreen's mother, Janet, had a very difficult time understanding why her daughter needed to do this. She faulted her own parenting and became angry at herself for not doing something to prevent Doreen from ever considering a search. Janet felt that she would have to share Doreen with another mother. She was devastated.

Janet gradually came to understand Doreen's need to find her roots. Once Janet realized that she would not be replaced, she became more supportive.

Both Doreen and Janet were dealing with their fears of being abandoned. Abandonment plays a large part in all adoptive families, and all adoptive parents and their children deal with it to some degree or another. Adopted children are afraid that their parents will leave them or give them up, somehow repeating the original relinquishment by their bioparents. Adoptive parents fear that they are only temporary parents and are easily expendable and will be replaced as soon as their children find their bioparents. Doreen was afraid that her mother would abandon her if she searched for her biofamily, and Janet feared that her daughter would leave her as soon as she found another mother, leaving Janet childless once again. Other adoptive parents and children have similar beliefs:

ALL OF THESE FEARS ARE IRRATIONAL AND ARE NOT FOUNDED ON FACT.

You and your children have solid relationships built from the ground up on firm structures of love, caring, and communication. By the time your children become adults, they will know that they can talk to you about anything, most particularly their adoption needs.

Follow these six steps when your adult children want to search:

1. LET THEM KNOW THAT YOU UNDERSTAND.
Repeat all that you have told them throughout their lives. You will always be there for them, no matter what.
2. TELL THEM THAT YOU WILL SUPPORT THEM.
Let them know that you will give them the emotional support they need at this time and always.
3. ASK THEM TO SHARE THEIR FEARS WITH YOU.
They are afraid of losing your love, of what they might find, of being rejected.
Help them talk about their feelings.
4. LISTEN TO WHAT THEY ARE TELLING YOU.
Do not make assumptions. Ask for clarification so that you can understand.
5. FIND OUT IF THEY NEED YOUR HELP IN OTHER WAYS.
They may want you to be actively involved in the process or to stay out of it completely. Respect their wishes.
6. BACK UP YOUR WORDS WITH ACTION.
Do not make idle statements with no follow-through.
They need you. Don't let them down.

Again, it is important to remember that not all adoptees want to actively search for their roots; however, all adoptees are curious. Your children, no matter what their age, regard you as their parents and will always think of you in that way, no matter how they may handle their curiosity:

YOU ARE THE TRUE PARENTS OF YOUR CHILDREN.

My eldest son made that very clear in a card he gave to me recently in which he said:

Chance made you my mother;
Love made you "Mom."

A daughter wrote the following words to her parents after searching for and finding her bioparents:

You're my REAL parents, Mom and Dad.
I love you and always will.

IV

Looking Back, Looking Ahead

VI

Looking Back,
Looking Ahead

14

The Bioparents

The promise of birth is a joyful event for most individuals. But the birth process is unknown to adoptive parents who are infertile. They can only experience the delight of the birth of a child from the wings, looking in but never able to fully participate. The hurts and longings that are very real for most adoptive parents are those you went through before you had your family. There have probably been times when you wished you had carried and given birth to your adopted children. But the reality for most of you is that you could not conceive or bear a child.

Bioparents also suffer in the adoption process. Most bioparents reach the decision to place their child after a long and difficult soul-searching. Very few women are able to cavalierly give up a baby who they have carried for nine months. The attachment formed during that period can last a lifetime. Biofathers must also come to terms with their decision, and many of them agonize over what they know they must do.

Many years ago when I was in the hospital for surgery, I met a young woman who was having a C-section. She had walked up to my room and began a conversation with me. I invited her in and after an hour of talk, she had learned about my adoptive family. She was reluctant to share much about herself, but finally began to talk. This was her first pregnancy. She was unmarried and when the baby was born, she was planning to place it for adoption. As she talked about her doubts and misgivings, tears began to well up in her eyes. Finally, she stood up, put her arms around me, and held me for a few minutes. Then she looked straight into my eyes and told me that I had helped relieve her concerns. It was clear to her that I deeply loved my children, and she was assured that her child would also be held dear by its adoptive family.

I never saw that woman again, but I have often thought of her, wondering about her and the child she relinquished and the couple whose lives were enriched because of that adoption. I told my own children about that woman and the love she felt for her child and her courage in making the decision. She helped to bring us all closer to my children's own bioparents.

Whenever my daughter and sons have a birthday, I think about their bioparents, where they might be, if they are also remembering at that very moment. In spirit, they are part of every occasion, every holiday and special time. As my children get older, I feel more connected to their biofamilies and wonder if I will ever meet them. They have given our family gifts for which I am forever grateful.

Many bioparents also speculate about the children they gave up, about where they are and whether they should have somehow tried to keep them. They often wait, hoping to be found some day by the children they had placed for adoption. Many of them continue to agonize over the decision, attempting to find a way that might have allowed them to keep their children. They feel cheated of the life that had been a part of them.

Bioparents will always be connected to adopted children and not only because of heredity. They are real people with genuine feelings. The decision that most of them made was out of love and bravery. These bioparents never forget the child they give up for adoption. The seeds they planted years before stay with them for a lifetime, and even though they did not tend and care for their baby, they can never forget their child.

The Biomother

Many of the biomothers who have consulted with me both before the adoption and many years later have expressed fears, doubts, and longings. The painful decision to place their child for adoption is usually made alone, sometimes in secrecy, with rarely any support, and sometimes with scorn, from their family and others.

The biomother is often viewed as uncaring; however, she is often the opposite. She is usually haunted by the decision she made earlier in her life. Many times she feels that she was forced to make up her mind by others who did not understand. She may carry anger and resentment about that period in her life when she experienced helplessness and when there were few persons who understood what she was feeling. Even though she made the decision to place her child for adoption, she wanted to believe that she had other options. She had hoped that someone else would save her from what she had to do.

One biomother told me that her actions have left her with powerful emotions that have never been resolved. When her child found her twenty-two years later, she realized that she had secretly been waiting and hoping for that moment, always believing that it would never be possible to have a chance to see her child again. To see him standing at her front door had been her fantasy, and then he was really there.

Many biomothers still wait to be found long after their children have become adults. They say that they do not want to disturb the adoptive family. Occasionally, they inform the adoption agency or attorney who arranged the adoption that they would be available if their children did want to meet them. Many bioparents are unaware of the fact that they can leave word of their availability. Often, though, they are afraid that they may be rejected or confronted in anger by their children. They believe that their children must hate them for placing them for adoption and that they could never be forgiven.

And so, they live with their dreams and fantasies.

Realities and Fantasies

Everyone involved in the adoption process has fantasies. As they speculate about one another, adoptive parents, adoptees, and bioparents alike share many thoughts in common. Their dreams about one another abound. The child who was relinquished is a mystery to the biomother, and she becomes an unanswered question for the adoptee and his or her adoptive parents. They may all continue to elude one another forever, or become very real people involved in a reunion.

Several years ago, one of my sons was a passenger in a car that was involved in an accident. As I sat with him in the middle of the night, first in the emergency room and then in the intensive care unit, I began to consider my son and our relationship. I looked at him, swollen, black and blue, barely able to talk. We waited for tests and X-rays to be completed; I was perched on a small footstool at the side of his bed. The emergency room was familiar. I had been there before . . . the time he nicked his chin—two stitches; a cut cheek—five stitches; the concussion when he jumped off a swing, and another when he fell out of a tree.

I found myself thinking of my son's biomother. He's hurt again. She would want to know. Could I tell her that he would be all right? If she had mothered him, would it have been different? Was I a good mother? Would she have been better for him?

I had all those questions and no answers.

I was feeling so inadequate and helpless about my son's condition that I began to have doubts about my abilities as a parent to carry out the responsibility of child-rearing that had been entrusted to me. I wanted to cry on his biomother's shoulder and have her console me.

While my son was recovering after surgery, I thought about his biomother again. He made it. He's going to be fine. We've weathered another storm. We did it without you, again. I found myself feeling both relief and anger.

My angry feelings came from being helpless about my son's condition and injuries and the lack of information to help me through the rough times, as if his biomother could have made it all better. Obviously, his biomother would have felt just as inadequate and would not have had the right answers either.

From time to time, most adoptive parents resent having so little information about their children, knowing that so much of what could be of assistance is held deep within the biofamilies. They hope that they can do a good job raising their children. There have probably been many times when you have felt ineffectual as a parent and hoped that you were adequate, even though your son or daughter was growing up missing a link to his or her biological heritage.

While you and the bioparents have your fantasies, your children will also dream.

The Ideal Mother

Although your children will feel a strong tie to you, they will still fantasize about their bioparents. They will have many questions: What do they look like? Where are they now? Are they thinking about me? Why did they give me up?

All youngsters, whether adopted or not, fantasize about an ideal parent—one who will always understand them, never discipline them, and meet their needs forever. We can all look back on our own childhood and remember times when we were angry at our parents for what we believed was an unjust reprimand. We imagined a "fairy godmother" who would appear and save us. Popular fairy tales confirmed and supported our illusions, and these stories are still read to young children everywhere.

For an adopted child, the ideal parent becomes the idealized biomother, who happens to be a real person. Adopted children have a more difficult time dealing with their parents, both fantasy and real, than do other children. As they try to come to terms with reality, they may believe that their biomother will appear and make everything all right. The imagined biomother has the potential of being the perfect parent.

Of course, your children know that you are their true parents—still, all children will dream. You can help them understand that there can never be a perfect mother, and, at the same time, allow them to express their feelings about their fantasies. Then they will be able to differentiate between what they have idealized and what is real.

The Biomother as a Threat

Adoptive parents will often fear the biomother. They are afraid that their child's biomother will come and sweep their son or daughter away from them. An adoptive mother once told me that she was concerned that her child would readily go with his biomother if he had a choice. Other parents have even talked about hiding or moving to another town to avoid this imagined threat.

When we explore their fears, we usually find that the adoptive parents feel insecure in their role as parents. Sometimes they feel envy of the biomother's child-bearing ability and even believe that their children would automatically choose a mother who was fertile. Although these fears may be unfounded, there are adoptive parents who do have such fears. As they gradually become more confident in their role as parents, they gain the ability to relax their concerns and become more assured, knowing that no one can ever take away the emotional bond that they have with their son or daughter. That attachment is unique.

As we discussed in chapter 12, these threats are more imagined than real; however, if you are a parent with these thoughts, they may seem very true to you. Just remember that fantasies and dreams are not reality.

Now let's see how the biofather fits into all of this.

The Biofather

When Steve placed his son for adoption, he thought he would never see him again. Over the years, Steve lost contact with his son's biomother, finished his schooling, and became a successful graphics artist. From time to time, he wondered how his son was doing and hoped that he was happy and well. Occasionally, Steve would feel a pang of remorse at not being able to raise his son. After a failed marriage, divorce, and no other children, Steve dreamed about his son even more. Then one day he received a phone call that changed everything.

He had just returned from a business trip when his son, Rick, called. Rick had tracked him down after first making contact with his biomother. Steve and Rick agreed to meet, and Steve made plans to fly to Chicago where Rick lived with his parents.

During the flight, Steve considered what he might

find when he arrived. He knew that he did not want to do anything to interfere with Rick's adoptive family and believed that Rick's adoptive parents were his true parents. He wondered how he would fit in.

When Steve got off the plane, it was not difficult to find his son in the crowd. The resemblance was remarkable. After introductions to Rick's parents, they all went back to Rick's home, where he had lived ever since the adoption twenty-three years before.

Steve learned about Rick, his personality, talents, and the fact that Rick was having some difficulty setting goals for himself. His father, an engineer, and his mother, a teacher, had provided Rick with many opportunities to develop his artistic aptitude, first in college and then at an art school. They had built a ceramics lab for him, complete with potter's wheel and kiln, but Rick was still restless, insecure.

When Rick decided to search for his bioparents, he did not know what he would find. He was scared and excited at the same time. His parents were supportive but gave him the space to search at his own pace. It took him two years to build up enough courage to begin and another two to actually find his biomother.

Now Rick had created an opportunity to learn more about himself. It would take Steve and Rick time to get to know one another and to define the relationship that was forming between them.

Not all searches and meetings with biofamilies are as positive as the one Rick and Steve experienced. They were both realistic about the fact that the best they can expect to accomplish is a friendship. Rick will also have the opportunity to understand his unique talents and may have more hope in becoming an accomplished, satisfied adult.

Rick's adoptive family has shown understanding and his parents have given him emotional support throughout the process. They know that they will always be his parents, but they have created a climate in which Rick can explore the possibility of a new friendship with Steve. Rick is relieved that his parents have been there for him, and he is looking ahead to try to clarify the part that Steve will play in his life.

The biofather is usually viewed as the one who abandoned the biomother, thus forcing her to relinquish her child. By not being available to support or marry the biomother, he is considered the person responsible for the placement. This is certainly so in most cases; however, more biofathers are becoming part of the early decision-making process. It is often required that both the biofather and biomother sign the relinquishment papers. If the biofather is unavailable, a specific procedure is followed to be sure that he is given every opportunity to come forth and claim his rights. There are also situations in which the biomother is determined to place the child for adoption even though the biofather does not agree. If he is not able to care for the child and the mother chooses not to, then they must ultimately decide on placement.

Many biofathers, like Steve, also think about the children they relinquished. Their memories can stay with them for a lifetime, and some of these men will institute a search themselves as soon as their son or daughter becomes an adult. If they do not seek their child out directly, they will go to agencies or attorneys and leave their names and addresses so that their children may find them. Sometimes they will join registries that are part of all search organizations. Biomothers and adoptees may also join these groups. Through the efforts and registries of search groups, many biofamilies have been united.

Adoptees who search for their bioparents have indicated that they feel a greater connection to the biomother, the person who carried them for nine months and actually gave birth to them. They have a natural curiosity about the biofather, wanting to know who he is and what he is like, but they do not feel attached to the biofather in the same way. Some adoptees even carry an unresolved anger and resentment toward their biofather, who might have left their biomother during pregnancy. They carry the same biases that society has toward all biofathers. There seems to be no room for the possibility that these men could care about the children they relinquished.

Some adoptees who meet their biofathers develop friendships with them; others go no further than a single meeting.

Although fewer adoptees seem to search for their biofathers, when contact is made, the results are similar to those with biomothers. The relationships vary, depending on what the adoptee finds. Usually friendships are formed when both the adoptee and the bioparent want to make it happen.

Again, it is important to keep in mind that most bioparents are respectful of the adoptive family and do not want to intrude upon them. They usually acknowledge that the adoptive parents are the true parents, and they only hope to have some contact with their biochildren. They are delighted to develop a friendship, but most bioparents do not think of themselves as the true parents.

The Triad

As we look at the triad in the adoption process, we see that adoptive parents, adoptees, and bioparents have a great deal in common. They have all experienced fear, pain, and longing. They have dealt with separation and understand the true meaning of loss; they have mourned their losses and moved on in their lives; they have carried the scars of the past with them. Their shared feelings bind them together in an everlasting relationship. Even if they never meet or look into one another's eyes, they may still be able to understand and accept, with compassion and respect, their special union.

15

So You're an Adoptive Grandparent

Grandparents have a special place in the hearts of all families. Their nurturing and love create confidence and hope in their children and grandchildren alike. That extra hug from a grandparent can make the hurts all better and the disappointments less intense. There is nothing quite like a grandparent's smile of encouragement and pride at a task well done or a major accomplishment. A grandparent's love is a treasured gift.

And now *you* have the opportunity to take the prized role of grandparent.

As adoptive grandparents, you will have a great deal in common with all other grandparents. You can, without censor, brag about your grandchildren, show their photos off, and discuss their remarkable progress. Everyone will expect you to boast and swell with pride and, no doubt, you will be ready to do just that.

Let's take a look at how you fit into the adoption story.

Your Feelings About Adoption

When your children first told you that they were going to adopt a child, you were probably surprised and possibly stunned by the information. After all, you never expected that your grandchildren would not be related by blood. So it took some time for you to reflect on the information and think about the fact that you would now be adoptive grandparents. You may have wondered what your role would be, how you would fit in, what you would tell your friends. Even now, you may worry about how you will talk about adoption, about the questions you might be asked and how you will answer them.

You may also feel a sense of loss. Your grandchildren will not look like you or be like you. They will not be able to perpetuate your family's genetic heritage. To help you find a place for yourselves in the adoption story, let's look at some of the questions you may have.

WHAT DOES ADOPTION MEAN TO YOU?

You might have known someone in your own family who was adopted, or perhaps a friend or neighbor had an adoptive family. Most likely, all that you know is based on what you hear from others or the media, and you have, no doubt, formed your own opinions and feelings about the subject. And those thoughts may not all be positive. Much of what you know may even be based on myth.

HOW CAN YOU WORK THROUGH YOUR OWN SENSITIVITIES AND COME TO A BETTER UNDERSTANDING OF ADOPTION?

- Confide in your spouse or another close relative about how you feel.
- Let your confidant communicate with you.
- Discuss your feelings and thoughts with the son or daughter who is about to adopt.
- Listen to what this son or daughter has to say to you about what is about to happen.
- Be open to the information you hear.
- Give your children the emotional support they may need. It's not easy for them, either.

As you learn more, you will become more comfortable with the subject of adoption. After all, adoption is something warm and loving, and you will come to know that the emotional bond you will have with your grandchildren will grow through your lifetime together. After you are informed, you can talk about adoption with knowledge and assurance. You will have the facts to allay your concerns.

WHEN WILL YOU BE TALKING ABOUT ADOPTION?

Other family members and your friends will be asking questions about your adopted grandchildren. Their curiosity will abound. It is important to remember that you are not obligated to reply to any queries that you do not want to answer. All of the information that you have concerning your grandchildren's biological families is private. Let the sample questions and answers in the early chapters of this book guide you.

It is quite possible that your son or daughter may choose not to share any information about your grandchildren's heritage with you. For many of you, it will be difficult not to know, but consider the following:

- Your children may decide that it is up to their children to discuss adoption in their own way, when they are ready.

and, more important,

- You can still be the very best grandparents possible, even without those facts.

Your grandchildren may attempt to engage you in conversation about their adoption. They may toss out a phrase about it or ask you a question. When they want to talk, let them. Just listen. If they ask you questions, suggest that they discuss anything about their adoption with their parents, whether you have the answers or not. Tell them that their own parents are the ones who can give them the facts they need. If they express any feelings that seem painful or difficult for them, help them by listening and then encourage them to talk to their parents. You may also want to let your son and daughter know if their children are having any concerns or questions about their adoption.

Your Role as Adoptive Grandparents

Once you have accepted the fact that your grandchildren are adopted, you can get on with your role as grandparent. You have learned that your son and daughter and their children are different from other families in some ways and similar in many others. They will be dealing with issues relating to adoption that will be new to them and to you, but your role as grandparent has little to do with adoption.

As grandparents, you will have a substantial effect on your family. Your children will look to you for your child-rearing expertise and your sound judgment. You have firsthand knowledge of what it is like to be a parent.

The friendship you have developed with your child as an adult will lay the groundwork for mutual respect and admiration. Your son or daughter will value your input when it is offered by one friend to another, not by parent to child. Developing the relationship you would like to have with your child will probably take some effort. It is not always easy to break old patterns that began years earlier.

Even if you have a good rapport with your children, you may find that they will not always follow your guidelines. When they make choices other than those you recommend, it may be difficult for you. You will have to watch them make mistakes, much as you did when they were youngsters, or, perhaps, they may teach you something new. What your children need to know is that you are there if they do need your support.

It will probably be very easy for you to nurture and encourage your grandchildren. They will have a unique relationship with you. Both of you will cherish the mutual love between you. You will be your grandchild's champion, ready to forgive and forget, understanding in a way that no one else is. Yours is a special love.

When You Don't Hit It Off with Your Grandchild

There may be times when you do not hit it off with one of your grandchildren. Even though you may try your best to make a deep connection, you may still find that you have difficulty. Your grandchild may feel the same way. Either your temperaments do not mesh or your personalities are too just too different. Whatever the reason, it is important for you as adoptive grandparents to know that other grandparents also may not be able to relate to their grandchildren. This can happen in biological as well as in adoptive families. Adoptive grandparents, however, may wonder whether their lack of affinity is based on the fact that their grandchild is adopted. Adoption has nothing to do with it.

Many of you may be afraid to admit that you are unable to relate to your grandchildren. Guilty and ashamed that you feel this way, as adoptive grandparents, you may want to cover up your feelings. Instead of chastising yourself, let's see what you can do.

When you are unable to get along with a grandchild:

- Acknowledge the way you feel.
- Explore your feelings in order to understand their cause.

The chances are that your feelings are not related to adoption, but if they are:

- Consult with someone who can help you get in touch with what is really bothering you.
- Become better informed about adoption.
- Forgive yourself for having the feelings.

Getting Acquainted

Keep these seven suggestions in mind as you prepare to get closer to your grandchildren:

1. Look at your grandchildren in the light of their unique talents and abilities.
2. Know that their strengths may not be yours.
3. Let them tell you about who they are.
4. Respect the differences between you.
5. Accept the disparities.
6. Believe that you cannot change them.
7. Value your grandchildren's specialness.

Now you are ready to enjoy and savor your role as a grandparent. Your experience and wisdom will go a long way to make the relationship you have with your adoptive family a memorable one. The affection you share with them will be a legacy of love to your family.

Epilogue

Yesterday, I was touched by a child
In a lifetime, a moment to savor
A fleeting taste of joy
Enriched with sweetest flavor.

Today, the touch is part of me
A memory, an instant, cool and refreshing
A puff of sheer delight
The scent renewed and lingering.

A touch to be with me always
A stroke of brilliance to last
Stimulating a spectrum of images
Of wistful reflections long past.

Yesterday, I was touched by a child.

Twenty-four years in the life of a family seems like a moment. Surely, just a minute ago, I held my daughter in my arms for the first time. Seconds later, our eldest son and our next son and our youngest son were there also.

As I look at our family portrait over the fireplace, I see all of the personalities reacting and interreacting in the special way that defines our family and no other. The portrait was done about eighteen years ago, but I can still feel the same pride and love that I knew then.

My daughter was seated next to me on the red velvet sofa, leaning against her dad, with her elbow resting on her brother's knee. Her shoes were off, and the white lace of her socks was peeking out from under her blue jeans. She never did like to wear shoes—still doesn't. At her fifth birthday party, she kept changing her shoes from black patent leather party shoes to tennis shoes. She finally gave up and took them off altogether.

My eldest son is seated on his dad's lap, with his blond hair just touching my husband's ear. He looks relaxed and comfortable, but at any moment he will jump down and run outdoors to play on the swing, or leap off the slide, or climb up into the orange tree and hide while he eats an orange. While I'm frantically looking for him, he will call down from the tree, "Hi, Mom. Want an orange?"

My second son is standing on the sofa, leaning against the back. He has a big smile for the artist. He still has his big, black eyes with long, black lashes and a dimple in each cheek. Pretty soon, he'll be running outside, looking for his brother. His brother will probably help him into the tree and share his orange with him. When I come by, he'll giggle and wave.

My youngest son is seated on my lap. He's watching the others and seems to be quite content. He would like to go out and play with his brothers, but he can't walk yet. Maybe tomorrow he'll be riding his tricycle, then going to school, then learning how to drive.

My husband and I can now look at each other, feeling the joy and pain, sadness and surprises that were, and will continue to be, the themes of our lives. As all parents, we will retain that role for our children, no matter how old we or they are. They will look to us for advice along the way, and they will continue to teach us. After all, we have learned a great deal from them through their growing years: compassion, patience, and a breadth and depth of experience beyond measure. We look forward to the future, anticipating a new dimension in our relationship.

The love and affection that embraced our young family has deepened over the years. Today, as we look at our adult children, we see people we not only love but also have a deep regard for. They are reaching out to their future, becoming the people they were meant to be. Even though there have been some difficult periods along with the pleasurable ones, my husband and I can look with excited anticipation to the years ahead. Our children have all of the resources, both learned and innate, to create productive, satisfying lives.

Our pride extends to our grandchildren, who are learning and teaching, growing and exploring as their parents did years ago. Who knows what the coming years will bring?

We can only contemplate in awe the infinite possibilities.

Appendix A:

Adoption Terms

Adopted child: The infant or child who is legally raised by nonbiological parents.

Adoptee: An *adopted child,* most often used when talking about an adult who was adopted as an infant or child.

Adoption: The process of placing a child with nonbiological parents to be legally raised by them.

Adoption agency: A public or private office that arranges and supervises the *placement* of children for *adoption.*

Adoption attorney: An attorney who helps to facilitate the *placement* of children for *adoption.*

Adoption worker: The representative of the agency who supervises the adoption process, also referred to as *case worker,* or *worker.*

Adoptive father: The legal father of the *adopted child.*

Adoptive mother: The legal mother of the *adopted child.*

Adoptive parent: The legal mother or father of the *adopted child.*

Amended birth certificate: The birth certificate that is issued after the *legal adoption,* showing the *adoptive parents* as the legal parents of the *adopted child.*

Biofather: The biological father of the *adopted child,* often referred to as the birthfather.

Biological heritage: The background of the *adopted child,* the family of origin.

Biological roots: The adopted child's *biological heritage.*

Biomother: The biological mother of the *adopted child,* often referred to as the birthmother.

Bioparent: The biological mother or father of the *adopted child,* often referred to as the birthparents.

Case worker: *See adoption worker.*

Final adoption: The legal act of officially naming the *adoptive parents* as the legal parents of the *adopted child.*

Genetic heritage: The hereditary background of the *adopted child.*

Home study: The process in which the *adoption worker* meets with the couple who will be adopting the child to determine their eligibility.

Infertility: The inability to conceive and give birth to biological children.

Legal adoption: *See final adoption.*

Nonidentifying information: Data about the *biological* and *genetic heritage* of the *adopted child,* not including names, addresses, or telephone numbers of the *bioparents* and their families.

Petition to adopt: The legal document filed with the court prior to the *legal adoption* of the child.

Placement: The act of relinquishing a child for *adoption.*

Relinquishment: The act of placing a child for *adoption.*

Reunion: A meeting between the adult *adoptee* and the *biomother* or *biofather* or both.

Sealed records: Identifying data and information about the *bioparents* that cannot be revealed except by a court order.

Search: The process by which the adult *adoptee* or *bioparent* looks for and tries to find the *bioparent* or child placed for *adoption,* respectively.

Triad: The three members of the adoption process: *adoptee, adoptive parent,* and *bioparent.*

Worker: *See adoption worker.*

Appendix B:

Support Organizations

The following support organizations are listed under their main offices or headquarters. Contact the main office for local chapters in your area.

There may be other support groups in your area. Contact public or private adoption agencies for information about specific local support organizations.

Adoption Triangle Ministry (ATM)
Box 1860
Cape Coral, FL 33910   (813) 542-1342

Alma Society (Adoptees' Liberty Movement Association)
P.O. Box 154
Washington Bridge Station
New York, NY 10033   (212) 581-1568

American Adoption Congress (AAC)
P.O. Box 44040
L'Enfant Station
Washington, DC 20026   (202) 638-1543

Committee for Single Adoptive Parents
P.O. Box 15084
Chevy Chase, MD 20815   (202) 966-6367

Concerned Persons for Adoption (CPFA)
P.O. Box 179
Whippany, NJ 07981   (201) 839-3340

Concerned United Birthparents (CUB)
595 Central Ave.
Dover, NH 03820   (603) 749-3744

Families Adopting Children Everywhere (FACE)
P.O. Box 28058
Northwood Station
Baltimore, MD 21239   (301) 799-2100

Holt International Children's Services (HICS)
P.O. Box 2880
Eugene, OR 97402   (503) 687-2202

International Concerns Committee For Children (ICCC)
911 Cypress Dr.
Boulder, CO 80303   (303) 494-8333

International Soundex Reunion Registry (ISRR)
P.O. Box 2312
Carson City, NV 89702   (702) 882-6270

Latin America Parents Association (LAPA)
P.O. Box 72
Seaford, NY 11783   (516) 752-0086

Michigan Association of Single Adoptive Parents (MASAP)
P.O. Box 601
Southfield, MI 48037   (313) 435-0816

National Adoption Exchange (NAE)
1218 Chestnut St.
Philadelphia, PA 19107   (215) 925-0500

National Committee for Adoption (NCFA)
1346 Connecticut Ave., NW
Washington, DC 20036   (202) 463-7559

North American Center on Adoption (NACA)
67 Irving Pl.
New York, NY 10003   (212) 254-7410

North American Council on Adoptable Children (NACAC)
810 18th St., NW, Suite 703
Washington, DC 20006   (202) 466-7570

Open Door Society, Adoption Warmline   (213) 402-3664

Operation Identity (OI)
13101 Blackstone Rd., NE
Albuquerque, NM 87111   (505) 293-3144

Orphan Voyage (OV)
Cedaredge, CO 81413   (303) 856-3937

Reunite, Inc.
P.O. Box 694
Reynoldsburg, OH 43068   (614) 861-2584

WAIF
67 Irving Pl.
New York, NY 10003   (212) 533-2558

Appendix C:

Suggested Readings

For the Preschooler

The following books can be read to the young child. The school-age child should be able to read them without your help. They are illustrated to enhance the stories.

Brodzinsky, Anne Braff. _The Mulberry Bird: Story of an Adoption._ Fort Wayne, Ind.: Perspectives Press, 1986. For the older preschooler (ages four to six). This loving story about a mother bird who must place her baby bird for adoption is told with sensitivity and warmth.

Koch, Janice. _Our Baby: A Birth and Adoption Story._ Fort Wayne, Ind.: Perspectives Press, 1985. For the older preschooler (ages four to six). This sex education book can help the young child understand birth and adoption. It is simple, straightforward, direct.

Lapsley, Susan. _I Am Adopted._ London: The Bodley Head, 1974. For very young children (ages two to four). This simple, warm story is told in the words of a young adopted boy.

For the School-age Child and Young Teenager

Klementz, Jill. _How It Feels to Be Adopted._ New York: Alfred A. Knopf, 1982. Personal accounts of adopted children. Each chapter is a separate story accompanied by individual and family photos.

Search and Reunion

Askin, Jayne, and Bob Oskam. *Search, a Handbook for Adoptees and Birth-parents.* New York: Harper & Row, 1982. For adult adoptees, their adoptive parents, and bioparents. Describes the process of search.

Lifton, Betty Jean. *Lost and Found, the Adoption Experience.* New York: Bantam, 1979. For adult adoptees, their adoptive parents, and bio-parents. Written by an adult adoptee who talks about her feelings about being adopted, her search experience, and those of others.

Bioparents

Silber, Kathleen, and Phyliss Speedlin. *Dear Birthmother: Thank You for Our Baby.* San Antonio, Tex.: Corona, 1983. For adoptive parents, bioparents, and adult adoptees. Addresses the feelings of adoptive parents and bioparents through letters and narrative.

General Information

Johnston, Patricia Irwin. *Perspectives on a Grafted Tree: Thoughts for Those Touched by Adoption.* Fort Wayne, Ind.: Perspectives Press, 1983. For the teenager, adult adoptee, adoptive parents, bioparents, and any-one touched by adoption. A collection of poetry about adoption.

Kirk, H. David. *Adoptive Kinship, a Modern Institution in Need of Reform.* Toronto: Bitterworth's, 1981. For anyone touched by adoption. Written by a sociologist who has conducted numerous research stud-ies with adoptive families.

Sorosky, Arthur D., Annette Baran, and Reuben Pannor. *The Adoption Triangle.* New York: Doubleday, 1978. For anyone touched by adop-tion. A comprehensive account of research studies, clinical experi-ences, and correspondence among adoptees, adoptive parents, and bioparents.

Index

seeing children as
humans, 73
seeing children as
separate individuals,
75–76
setting limits for
adolescents, 132–135
setting unrealistic goals
for children and
themselves, 72–73
as teachers, 106, 121
understanding children's
feelings about adoption,
148
Peers, in lives of
adolescents, 107, 117
Physically handicapped
child, adopting, 68
Pregnancy, children's
questions about, 34
Preschool "toddler" years,
31–41
adopting toddlers, 38–41
child's own adoption
story, 31–34
child's questions about
adoption, 34–37
child's questions about
infertility, 35
child's questions about
pregnancy, 34
emotional and
psychological bonds,
33
expectations for, 84
inquisitiveness in, 31
questions from others
about adoption, 37–38
Professional help, seeking,
87–89
Psychological theory,
71

Puberty, 101–115
boys in, 105
girls in, 105
mood swings in, 106
peer groups and, 107
physical changes in,
104–109
growth spurts, 104–105
relationships in, 107–108
sexuality and, 109–111
teeter-totter of, 108–109
unpredictability of,
102–103

Relinquishment
biofather's role in, 176
causes of, 9
fears of, 163
society's attitudes toward,
9
Reproduction, 3–7
biological motivation for, 5
fertility and, 3–5

School years, 42–53
adopting school-age child,
52–53
adoption talk, 50–52
anger, 53
arrival of new child, 58
feelings of other people
about adoption, 48–49
helping child accept
himself in spite of
limitations, 47–48
learning abilities, 45
learning disabilities,
45–46
leaving safety of home,
43–44
peers' effect during, 43
separaton anxiety, 43–44

About the Author

Dr. Stephanie E. Siegel is an adoptive mom. A psychotherapist who specializes in adoption, she has appeared on TV talk shows ("Woman to Woman," "Careers," "Solutions") and has been interviewed for radio on "It's Your Affair" and Los Angeles' KGIL's "Weekend Magazine." Her column on parenting appeared monthly in *Women's News*.

Using her own experience with a family of four children (three of whom are adopted), Dr. Siegel brings personal identification as well as professional skills to her work with families who meet the ever-changing demands of adoption. She counsels both individuals and groups and offers help to bioparents considering relinquishment, infertile couples, couples waiting for a child, adoptive parents and families, adopted children, adult adoptees, and adoptees and bioparents during search and reunion.

Often her services extend into the community. As Director of Family Life Education at the Congregational Church in Northridge, California, Dr. Siegel developed workshops for parents. She currently leads three adoptive parent support groups and has led a single parent bereavement group at Stephen S. Wise Temple in Los Angeles. In addition, she has lectured extensively in the Southern California area on subjects related to adoption and parenting.

Dr. Siegel maintains her professional practice and supervises interns at the Valley Counseling Clinic in Van Nuys, California.

She also has a license to practice counseling and therapy in Montana. She earned her bachelor of arts degree at the University of California, Los Angeles, got her master's degree from the California Graduate Institute, and received her Ph.D. in clinical psychology and adoption from International College in Los Angeles. As a member of both the American Association for Marriage and Family Therapists and the California Association of Marriage and Family Therapists, she has been actively involved in the San Fernando Valley chapter. Dr. Siegel lives in the San Fernando Valley with her husband and two of their four children.